The Reference Shelf®

Hispanic Americans

Edited by Paul McCaffrey

Editorial Advisor Lynn M. Messina

The Reference Shelf
Volume 79 • Number 1

The H.W. Wilson Company
2007

The Reference Shelf

The books in this series contain reprints of articles, excerpts from books, addresses on current issues, and studies of social trends in the United States and other countries. There are six separately bound numbers in each volume, all of which are usually published in the same calendar year. Numbers one through five are each devoted to a single subject, providing background information and discussion from various points of view and concluding with a subject index and comprehensive bibliography that lists books, pamphlets, and abstracts of additional articles on the subject. The final number of each volume is a collection of recent speeches, and it contains a cumulative speaker index. Books in the series may be purchased individually or on subscription.

Library of Congress has cataloged this serial title as follows:

Hispanic Americans / edited by Paul McCaffrey.
   p. cm. — (The reference shelf ; v. 79, no. 1)
     Includes bibliographical references and index.
   ISBN 978-0-8242-1067-0 (alk. paper)
   1. Hispanic Americans—Social conditions. 2. Immigrants—United States—Social conditions. 3. Hispanic Americans—Politics and government. 4. Hispanic Americans—Economic conditions. 5. Hispanic Americans—Education. 6. United States—Social conditions—1980– 7. United States—Ethnic relations. I. McCaffrey, Paul, 1977–
   E184.S75H5653 2007305.8968'073—dc22

                                           2006100239

Visit H.W. Wilson's Web site: www.hwwilson.com

Printed in the United States of America

Contents

Preface

Like any racial or ethnic category, the designation Hispanic American often obscures more than it reveals, blurring distinctions between races, languages, economic classes, and countries of origin. Indeed, the term can describe a person with white, black, indigenous, or mixed ancestry; a Spanish, English, or Guarani speaker; a Cuban exile in Miami, a Mexican American in Southern California, or a Dominican in New York City. Given the sheer breadth of this diversity, any analysis that proposes to present a complete picture of the Hispanic-American community will likely come up short. Nevertheless, the articles contained in this collection were chosen to provide as accurate and full a portrait of the American Latino as possible, combining the demographic figures—the hard numbers—with a more personal exploration of the cultural aspects of the community.

The first chapter offers an overview of the Hispanic-American experience, providing a demographic profile while charting the myriad regional, linguistic, and ethnic variations that exist within it. Particular emphasis is given to the American West, where Mexican Americans have well-established ties; Florida, where the Cuban community has long been ascendant; and New York City, with its melting pot of Puerto Ricans, Dominicans, and other Latinos. Coverage is also given to a locale not often associated with Hispanic immigration: a sleepy town in the Appalachian Mountains of Tennessee. Indeed, as their numbers grow, Latinos are becoming increasingly rural.

As with previous immigrant waves, the influx of Hispanics has engendered a backlash in certain sectors of the population: Anger over undocumented workers, who some believe drive down wages, and fears of permanent changes to the nation's cultural and ethnic makeup have led to a vociferous debate as to just how welcoming the country ought to be toward these new immigrants. Entries in the second chapter explore these controversies from a range of perspectives.

Articles in the third section analyze the expanding political clout of Hispanic voters. While many consider Hispanics, like Irish, Italian, and Jewish immigrants before them, a traditional Democratic constituency, Republicans have made inroads among Latino voters in recent elections, proving, at the very least, that neither party can afford to take their support for granted.

The fourth chapter charts the rapid ascendance of Hispanics in the economic and cultural spheres of American life. From the Internet, to music, to television and the movies, Latinos are leaving an ever greater imprint on American entertainment and commerce.

Entries in the final chapter focus on the education of Hispanic Americans, considering the debate over bilingual education, the importance of early childhood education for Hispanic toddlers, the history of segregation and integration of Hispanic students, and college attendance and graduation rates for Hispanics.

In conclusion, I would like to thank the many authors and publishers who have granted permission to reprint the articles contained in this book. I would also like to extend my gratitude to the many friends and colleagues at the H.W. Wilson Company who contributed their time and talent to this endeavor, particularly Richard Stein and Lynn Messina.

Paul McCaffrey
February 2007

I. The Hispanic-American Experience: Demographics and Beyond

Editor's Introduction

Given the size and diversity of the Hispanic-American population, it can be difficult—not to mention counterproductive—to generalize about it. Therefore, the first chapter in this collection will provide as broad and multidimensional a portrait of the Latino community as possible, taking into account the considerable demographic, geographic, linguistic, and cultural variations that exist within it.

The first selection, "Latino? Hispanic? Chicano?" by Juan Castillo, addresses the classification issue: Among Latinos there is considerable disagreement over what term to use to refer to themselves. As Castillo illustrates, some find "Hispanic" offensive and prefer to use "Latino," which is likewise viewed as derogatory in some quarters.

Moving beyond the classification controversy, the next piece, "Hispanic Americans," by Roberto Suro, offers a general overview of the Latino community while also noting the evolution that is taking place as Hispanics, who were once located in specific major cities and geographical areas, have spread across the country. Suro likewise highlights the generational gaps that exist within the community. Featured as sidebars in the article are three tables from the Pew Hispanic Center that offer a statistical blueprint of the Hispanic community, charting the population by birthplace, country of origin, and location by state.

Hispanics occupy a singular place in the American racial milieu. In Latin America the rates of intermarriage between indigenous peoples, white settlers, and African immigrants were considerably greater than in the United States. Consequently there is a broad spectrum of racial categories that makes the typical black/white designation imprecise, as Chris Echegaray observes in "Racial, Ethnic Identities Evolve as Nation Changes."

Just as Hispanics contribute to racial diversity in the United States, they likewise add a degree of linguistic variety to American speech. In "A Hybrid Tongue or Slanguage?" Daniel Hernandez explores the emergence of a distinct dialect among American Hispanics that combines elements of both English and Spanish. Another sidebar from the Pew Hispanic Center details the rate of English usage among Latinos.

The Anglo-Irish author George Bernard Shaw described England and the United States as "two nations divided by a common language." In many ways this is true of American Hispanics, who aside from sharing a language, may have little else in common with one another. Seth Kugel illustrates this point in "The Latino Culture Wars," as he describes the disparate Latino communities that exist side by side in New York City, one of the major hubs of Hispanic Americans in the United States.

Along with New York City, the American West and Southwest—particularly Texas and California—as well as the state of Florida have historically high concentrations of Latinos, with their origins in the Spanish colonial era. The next several entries examine the Hispanic communities in these particular locales. Sarah Coppola, in "Hispanics Have Made Great Strides But Are Still Striving," offers a multifaceted glimpse of Mexican-American life in Texas, while Felix F. Gutierrez provides a historical and personal portrait of the Chicano experience in California, in "The House That Used to Be in Mexico." One of the more significant Latino populations in the United States is the Cuban community of Florida, many of whose members migrated from their homeland as a reaction against Fidel Castro's revolution. Recent immigration from other nations, however, has made the Latino population of Florida much more diverse, as John-Thor Dahlburg reports in "Changes in Rhythm for Florida."

Though most Hispanic Americans in the United States continue to live in the regions mentioned above, more and more are settling in areas not often associated with such diversity. In the last entry in this chapter, "The New Face of Appalachia," Kim Cobb visits the community of Morristown, Tennessee, in the Appalachian Mountains, where the Latino population is swelling, as it is throughout the American South and across the country.

Latino? Hispanic? Chicano?

By Juan Castillo
Austin American-Statesman, July 26, 2003

Hispanic or Latino?

What is the proper name for the 38.8 million people of Latin American origin who live in this country—43 million if you add Puerto Rico?

The National Council of La Raza, which brought together 22,000 Hispanic—or is it Latino?—leaders to Austin this month, says it can live with both terms. "We've got so many real important issues to work on, we don't spend a lot of time nit-picking over this," says Lisa Navarrete of the council.

She acknowledges that the question "inspires fiery debate" and unleashes strong regional preferences, which the council tries to respect.

"Here in Texas, I know people prefer Hispanic," she says.

Though the U.S. government began using the term Hispanic more than 20 years ago, there is no consensus among the millions of people the label was intended to represent. Even the government now uses the terms Latino and Hispanic interchangeably for the largest minority group in a country of 288.4 million people.

The debate won't go away, though some clearly wish it would. Choosing an identity—Latino or Hispanic or something else—resonates with social, political, geographical and generational meaning. It inspires personal stands and, at times, strenuous, impassioned objections.

Author and poet Sandra Cisneros, who wrote "Caramelo" and "The House on Mango Street," is sensitive to the resonance of words. Don't call her Hispanic. She's offended by the term, so much so that Hispanic magazine says she refused to be on its cover. Eventually, she changed her mind and in September 2002 appeared on the cover on her terms: sporting a large cauldron-and-flames tattoo on her left bicep that reads, "Pura Latina."

"The term Hispanic makes my skin crawl," Cisneros told the magazine, which uses Latino and Hispanic interchangeably. "It's a very colonistic term, a disrespectful term, a term imposed on us without asking what we wanted to call ourselves."

She prefers Latina, Chicana, Tejana and Mexican American.

But some find the term Latino just as objectionable. And others, like author Richard Rodriguez, find the debate tiresome.

POLL THE PEOPLE

A December 2000 poll for HISPANIC magazine found that a majority of people of Latin American origin preferred the term Hispanic. Hispanic Trends Inc. polled 1,200 Latino registered voters in the United States. Sixty-five percent preferred Hispanic and 30 percent chose to identify themselves as Latino. The survey also found that 67 percent of Mexican Americans in Texas preferred the term Hispanic. "We thought we had pretty much resolved the issue and, of course, it's not," said Carlos Verdecia, editor of HISPANIC magazine.

"My own preference is for Hispanic, only because it gets to the complexity of what it is to be related to Latin America," says Rodriguez, who wrote "Brown: The Last Discovery of America". "It gets to the predicament of many of us that we come from a Spanish-speaking world, but are living in an English world. It gets to our confusion, our potential vitality of a people. We have two memories of ourselves. But finally, I'm just finding that the debate is less and less interesting."

Rodolfo de la Garza, vice president of the Tomas Rivera Policy Institute and a political scientist at Columbia University, says the ongoing battle "has lost any utility."

"The Latino advocates point out that Hispanic doesn't include the Indian heritage and they're not Spanish. . . . (But) It's not clear that a person who calls himself Hispanic is any politically different than a person who calls himself Latino."

At the La Raza advocacy group's conference in Austin, it was easy to find the spectrum of preferences—not always aligned with the view that in Texas the preferred term is Hispanic.

"Our Spanish roots go so far back, it's so removed and such a different culture," says Austin's Sonia Montejano, 19, a student at Stanford University. She prefers to be called Latina or Mexicana or Chicana.

Montejano and her mother, Margarita Decierdo, a sociologist who prefers to call herself a Latina or a Chicana, echo a common refrain: Hispanic is a term that was given to people, not the identity they chose.

But Jose Limon, the director for the Center for Mexican American Studies at the University of Texas, says the term Hispanic seems to be taking hold in Texas, particularly in the past five years. "The average person on the street of Mexican origin who is a U.S. citizen appears to be preferring to be called Hispanic in English," says Limon.

"My suspicion is that when referring to themselves in Spanish, they prefer 'Mexicano,'" Limon says.

An Old Debate

Austin's Maria Martin, who founded the nationally syndicated radio program "Latino USA," was asking the same question—Hispanic or Latino?—on other radio shows more than 30 years ago. The question and its persistence have to do with finding an identity in this country, says Martin, also the executive producer of the program, which chronicles Latino life and culture.

When "Latino USA" started 10 years ago, "we knew that we had to create a program that in some way transcended differences, but at the same time gave people a national identity," she says. "Many of us on the staff at that time felt and we still feel that the word Hispanic in some way pasteurizes who we are, and Latino at least has the ring of culture and the ring of language."

Hispanic first came into wide usage in the 1980s when the Census Bureau found it had undercounted people of Latin American heritage in the 1970 census. The term became the government's way to classify a disparate group of people—Puerto Ricans, Cubans, Mexican migrants, Spanish descendants—who already used many terms to refer to themselves. "Little wonder that the imposition of the official term Hispanic spawned controversy almost immediately," wrote Frank del Olmo, an associate editor with the Los Angeles Times.

The term also has been criticized for emphasizing the role of European influences in shaping ethnic identity to the neglect of indigenous cultures.

In the late 1970s, del Olmo and two other Times reporters were asked to examine what Latinos in Los Angeles called themselves. Their research was the precursor to the Times' adopting a guide on how to refer to its Latino population.

Mexican Americans, or simply Mexicans, was the preferred name for most Los Angelenos of Latin American origin, the reporters found. The catch-all term used to refer to other Latin Americans was Latino.

Words Alone

THE OXFORD ENGLISH DICTIONARY traces the word Hispanic to the 16th century, when it referred to residents of the Iberian Peninsula who spoke either Spanish or Portuguese. The word Latino dates to the 18th century and the colonial rivalry between England and France. "Its application to Latin Americans . . . was used to differentiate the 'Latin' world (France, Spain, Portugal, Italy and the many countries of Central America and South America, all of them predominantly Roman Catholic) from the English-speaking and largely Protestant world of Great Britain and its colonies in North America."

Source: "Latinos in the United States: A Resource Guide for Journalists"

The La Raza advocacy group used the term Hispanic almost exclusively, because much of the data the group generated was based on government numbers. "Then, a few years ago, we noticed that the word Latino had caught on. If you look at our publications (today), it's about a 50-50 mix," says Navarrete. "And for us, it refers to exactly the same group of people."

And who are they? "It's a self-identifier," Navarrete says. "People who trace their roots back to the Iberian Peninsula in some respect. There are Latinos who have very strong indigenous roots, African roots, but the commonality is tracing their roots back to the Iberian Peninsula."

Del Olmo uses the term Latino but is not wed to one term and is comfortable calling himself a Chicano. In the Southwest in the last century, Chicano came to refer to Mexicans living in the United States either as citizens or refugees from the Mexican Revolution.

He wonders if the term Latino caught on for a reason having nothing to do with identity and pride.

"It could be simply that the word Latino rolls more easily off the tongue of Spanish speakers than an English word like Hispanic," del Olmo says.

But Limon at UT thinks Hispanic has its own aural appeal. "It's a sexier, smoother, more suave way to identify yourself." Limon, who is working on a book on the Hispanic middle class, says that in Texas, doctors, attorneys and professional people are becoming more comfortable with the term Hispanic. "But you also see it used heavily among the working class."

CENSUS SENSES

The term Hispanic first appeared on a census form in 1980 when the government asked: "Is this person of Spanish/Hispanic origin or descent?"

- Hispanics or Latinos are those people who classified themselves in one of the specific Spanish, Hispanic or Latino categories listed on the Census 2000 questionnaire—"Mexican, Mexican American, Chicano," "Puerto Rican" or "Cuban"—as well as those who indicate that they are "other Spanish/Hispanic/Latino."

- People who said they are "other Spanish/Hispanic/Latino" include those whose origins are from Spain, the Spanish-speaking countries of Central or South America, the Dominican Republic or people identifying themselves generally as Spanish, Spanish-American, Hispanic, Hispano, Latino and so on.

- People who identify their origin as Spanish, Hispanic or Latino may be of any race.

Source: U.S. Census Bureau

Labels and Boxes

Should there be one term to describe people of Latin American origin?

"There is no one correct term, politically or substantively," says de la Garza, who points out that the Census adopted Hispanic with the help of a committee of Mexican Americans and other Spanish speakers. "Both terms are created. Hispanic is created and Latino is created. They're trying to construct an identity. That's what it's about."

Author Rodriguez wonders if categories and labels are out of step with the fluidity of the language of identity.

"These labels should be a way to identify our complexity," he says, "rather than a way to sort of freeze our identity."

"The kids in L.A. are renaming themselves more brownly even than (Latino or Hispanic)," he says. "They're calling themselves Blaxicans (as a way to describe their African and Latin American origin). The old Chicano was saying, 'We are border people.' The Latino is saying, 'We are no longer just Chicanos, but now related to Salvadorans and now belong to this new

> ### WORDS IN USE
>
> A sampling of what some organizations call themselves:
>
> - Latino USA
> - HISPANIC Magazine
> - LATINA Magazine
> - LATINA STYLE Magazine
> - Greater Austin Hispanic Chamber of Commerce
> - Association for the Advancement of Mexican Americans
> - Center for Mexican American Studies (University of Texas)
> - League of United Latin American Citizens
> - Mexican American Legal Defense and Education Fund
> - Hispanic Scholarship Fund
> - The Congressional Hispanic Caucus Institute
> - National Association of Latino Elected and Appointed Officials
> - Mexican American Hispanic Caucus (Texas House of Representatives)

union of Latin America'; the Hispanic is saying something else, the Blaxican is saying, 'We are also children of Africa.' And at every stage I hear the language is getting broader."

De la Garza sees a potential and lamentable social consequence in all of this wrangling over labels.

"What would be a tragedy is if you eliminate cultural distinctiveness under the creation of a single label that you're putting together for political reason." He sees it happening in New York, where a Hispanic heritage event celebrates Dies y Seis de Septiembre. "Well, that's a Mexican holiday. . . . It's not a Colombian holiday or an Argentine holiday.

"You talk about the Hispanic language. What the hell is that?"

He worries that history of national origin will be eliminated in the name of a uniform history. In the meantime, the landscape of national origins is rapidly changing—and mixing—as Salvadorans,

Hondurans, Colombians, Dominicans, and Guatemalans and their Latin American compatriots begin to live alongside each other. "In time you are really creating a new mixed identity that might best be called Latino or Hispanic. And the meaning at that time will be very different from the meaning that people attach to the debate today," he says.

Hispanic Americans

By Roberto Suro
World Almanac & Book of Facts, 2005

A Growing Minority

Think of a teenager who is growing fast, changing in appearance and forming a distinct identity all at once. That, roughly speaking, is where the Hispanic population of the U.S. finds itself today—in a kind of demographic adolescence. It is already an important member of the American family, but its ultimate character and impact are still to be determined.

The growth became stunningly apparent when the 2000 Census reported that the Hispanic or Latino (I use the terms interchangeably) population had grown to 35.3 million, a 58% jump from 1990, and the growth continues. The Census Bureau projects a Hispanic population of 47.8 million by the end of this decade. If that holds, the number of Latinos will grow nearly 6 times faster than the rest of the population.

Growth Around the Country

As it grows the Latino population is changing in character, starting with the places it calls home. For decades, Latinos have been concentrated in a handful of big cities, but they are now scattering across the country as well. In 2000, the greater metropolitan areas of Los Angeles, New York, Chicago, and Miami alone were home to 1 in 3 Latinos, but extraordinarily fast growth was occurring elsewhere in places where the Hispanic presence had been negligible. Between 1980 and 2000, Atlanta experienced a 995% increase in its Latino population. In Portland, OR, it grew by 437%, in Washington, DC, by 346%, and in Tulsa, OK, by 303%.

For the most part, these new destinations attracted Latinos, especially immigrants, because they offered jobs and affordable housing. Indeed, fast-paced economic development on a local level and rapid growth of the Latino population have gone hand-in-hand in places where Spanish was rarely heard a few decades ago. This trend has continued and may even have accelerated during the economic downturn of 2001–2002 and its aftermath. Hispanic population growth has become a national phenomenon affecting virtually every corner of the country.

Population by Race and Ethnicity: 2000 and 2005					
Universe: 2000 and 2005 Household Population					
	2005 population	2000 population	Percent of 2005	Percent change 2000-2005	Share of total change (%)
Hispanic	41,926,302	34,494,801	14.5	21.5	50.3
Native Born	25,085,528	20,488,299	8.7	22.4	31.1
Foreign Born	16,840,774	14,006,502	5.8	20.2	19.2
White alone, not Hispanic	192,526,952	189,520,003	66.8	1.6	20.4
Black alone, not Hispanic	34,410,656	32,036,110	11.9	7.4	16.1
Asian alone, not Hispanic	12,331,128	9,893,205	4.3	24.6	16.5
Other, not Hispanic	7,203,781	7,693,277	2.5	-6.4	-3.3
Total	288,398,819	273,637,396	100.0	5.4	100.0
Note: "Other, not Hispanic" includes persons reporting single races not listed separately and those reporting more than one race					
Source: Pew Hispanic Center tabulations of 2000 Census and 2005 American Community Survey					

© 2005 Pew Hispanic Center, a Pew Research Center project, www.pewhispanic.org.

Newcomers and Old-Timers

Nevertheless, Hispanics remain a relatively small share of the population. In 2000 they were about 13% of the total, and even with projections of rapid growth they will make up only 20% by 2030. It is not sheer size that determines the impact of the Hispanic population, but the fact that this segment of the population is growing so fast while the rest is growing hardly at all. To understand the dynamics of that growth and its significance, it is important to break down the Hispanic population into 3 key components:

- The new immigrants: Although people from Latin America have come to the U.S. during other periods, an unprecedented wave of migration from Spanish-speaking lands has been underway since the 1960s, and it has gained considerable momentum since the early 1990s. Currently, the Census Bureau estimates that migration, both legal and unauthorized, adds nearly 700,000 Latinos to the population each year. Many factors help determine the size of that flow and whether it will continue at the same rate. But as a result of the influx thus far, the foreign-born constitute about 40% of the Hispanic population.

- The second generation: Like most immigrants through history, new Hispanic immigrants have tended to be young adults of child-bearing age. Moreover, they have proved highly fertile, with birth rates almost twice as high as among non-Hispanic whites. As a result, there is now a huge second generation of Latinos— about 12.5 million people—that is very young, with a median age of about 13. They are the children of immigrants, but are full-fledged, native-born U.S. citizens. They now make up about 30% of the Hispanic population, and are the fastest-growing component.

- The old stock: Many Latinos lived in the U.S. before the current era of immigration began, and many trace their ancestry to families that lived in places like Texas, California, and Puerto Rico before those lands became part of the U.S. This component accounts for about 30%.

For the past 3 decades or so, the new immigrants have transformed urban neighborhoods, spurred the rise of Spanish-language media, and prompted periodic, sometimes heated, debates on immigration policy. Like many other immigrants, the Latino newcomers have not simply broken off ties with their home countries, but instead share their earnings with families left behind. The individual amounts are small, averaging about $300, but they are sent faithfully by a sizeable share of the immigrant population. These so-called remittances, totaling around $30 billion a year, have become an important factor in the economies of many Latin American nations. Meanwhile, in the U.S. the steady, growing supply of Latino immigrant workers has become a mainstay of several industries, such as construction and food processing. But even as the immigrant influx continues, the impact of Latino population growth is changing because the very makeup of that population is changing.

Second-Generation Hispanics

The second generation is the demographic echo of all that immigration, and it is a booming echo. Between 2000 and 2030 it will grow by about 17.7 million. Over the next 25 years or so, the number of second-generation Latinos in U.S. schools will double and the number in the labor force will triple. Nearly one-fourth of all labor force growth will be from children of Latino immigrants. The flow of newcomers from abroad is likely to continue, but even so the effect of Latino population growth is now shifting. Over the next several decades, the largest impact is going to be felt first in the nation's schools and then in the economy, as this unique group of Americans comes of age.

Latinos of the second generation differ markedly from their immigrant parents in several ways. They are not only native-born U.S. citizens but also native-born English speakers. While nearly three-quarters of the adults in the immigrant generation predominately speak Spanish, all but a small fraction of the second generation have mastered English. Moreover, the second generation is getting much more education than the immigrant generation, with almost twice as large a share going to college. Nonetheless, children of Latino immigrants lag behind non-Hispanic youth in every measure of educational achievement. And, they are different from other Ameri-

Hispanic Population by Nativity: 2000 and 2005					
Universe: 2000 and 2005 Hispanic Household Population					
	2005 population	2000 population	Percent Hispanic 2005	Percent change 2000-2005	Share of total change (%)
Native Born	25,085,528	20,488,299	59.8	22.4	61.9
Foreign Born	16,840,774	14,006,502	40.2	20.2	38.1
Total	41,926,302	34,494,801	100.0	21.5	100.0
Source: Pew Hispanic Center tabulations of 2000 Census and 2005 American Community Survey					

Detailed Hispanic Origin: 2005		
Universe: 2005 Hispanic Household Population		
	Number	Percent of Hispanic
Mexican	26,784,268	63.9
Puerto Rican	3,794,776	9.1
Cuban	1,462,593	3.5
Dominican	1,135,756	2.7
Costa Rican	111,978	0.3
Guatemalan	780,191	1.9
Honduran	466,843	1.1
Nicaraguan	275,126	0.7
Panamanian	141,286	0.3
Salvadoran	1,240,031	3.0
Other Central American	99,422	0.2
Argentinean	189,303	0.5
Bolivian	68,649	0.2
Chilean	105,141	0.3
Colombian	723,596	1.7
Ecuadorian	432,068	1.0
Peruvian	415,352	1.0
Uruguayan	51,646	0.1
Venezuelan	162,762	0.4
Other South American	89,443	0.2
Spaniard	362,424	0.9
All Other Spanish/Hispanic/Latino	3,033,648	7.2
Total	41,926,302	100.0

Source: Pew Hispanic Center tabulations of 2005 American Community Survey

cans, even other Hispanics, who are farther removed from the immigrant experience. Nearly half of second-generation Hispanics are bilingual, and many retain a degree of identification with their parents' home countries.

Their influence will be greatly magnified by an extraordinary historical coincidence: They will be moving into the workforce just as the huge Baby Boom generation of non-Hispanics is moving out.

Hispanic Population by State: 2000 and 2005			
Universe: 2000 and 2005 Hispanic Household Population			
	2005	2000	Change 2000-2005	Percent change 2000-2005
California	12,534,628	10,741,711	1,792,917	16.7
Texas	7,882,254	6,530,459	1,351,795	20.7
Florida	3,433,355	2,623,787	809,568	30.9
New York	3,026,286	2,782,504	243,782	8.8
Illinois	1,807,908	1,509,763	298,145	19.7
Arizona	1,679,116	1,267,777	411,339	32.4
New Jersey	1,312,326	1,098,209	214,117	19.5
Colorado	895,176	718,956	176,220	24.5
New Mexico	827,940	746,555	81,385	10.9
Georgia	625,382	425,305	200,077	47.0
Nevada	557,370	389,336	168,034	43.2
Washington	546,209	434,747	111,462	25.6
North Carolina	544,470	367,390	177,080	48.2
Massachusetts	489,662	412,496	77,166	18.7
Pennsylvania	488,144	381,159	106,985	28.1
Virginia	440,988	324,314	116,674	36.0
Michigan	378,232	318,285	59,947	18.8
Connecticut	372,718	309,798	62,920	20.3
Oregon	360,000	267,017	92,983	34.8
Maryland	311,191	227,586	83,605	36.7
Indiana	273,004	210,189	62,815	29.9
Utah	264,010	197,315	66,695	33.8
Ohio	253,014	212,007	41,007	19.3
Wisconsin	230,715	187,205	43,510	23.2
Oklahoma	218,987	168,944	50,043	29.6
Kansas	218,244	182,827	35,417	19.4
Minnesota	185,464	139,259	46,205	33.2
Tennessee	171,890	113,610	58,280	51.3
Missouri	154,744	114,741	40,003	34.9
South Carolina	136,616	90,263	46,353	51.4
Idaho	135,733	97,765	37,968	38.8
Arkansas	130,328	82,155	48,173	58.6
Louisiana	126,856	107,541	19,315	18.0
Nebraska	124,504	90,881	33,623	37.0
Rhode Island	114,077	87,454	26,623	30.4
Hawaii	103,764	84,471	19,293	22.8
Iowa	102,047	77,968	24,079	30.9
Alabama	98,624	70,305	28,319	40.3
Kentucky	65,177	53,002	12,175	23.0
Delaware	50,007	37,185	12,822	34.5
Mississippi	48,795	34,543	14,252	41.3
District of Columbia	43,856	42,913	943	2.2
Wyoming	36,722	28,769	7,953	27.6
Alaska	29,219	23,992	5,227	21.8
New Hampshire	24,248	20,740	3,508	16.9
Montana	21,970	18,113	3,857	21.3
Maine	12,407	10,074	2,333	23.2
South Dakota	12,311	9,399	2,912	31.0
North Dakota	11,380	7,020	4,360	62.1
West Virginia	9,760	12,310	-2,550	-20.7
Vermont	4,474	4,687	-213	-4.5
Total	41,926,302	34,494,801	7,431,501	21.5

Source: Pew Hispanic Center tabulations of 2000 Census and 2005 American Community Survey

Moreover, the Baby Boom did not produce a lot of children to take its place. According to Census Bureau projections, in 2004 there were 44 million non-Hispanics between 40 and 50, boomers heading toward retirement, but only 35 million who were 10 or younger to replace them. The gap will be filled by some 9 million Latinos 10 or younger. Latinos, especially the children of immigrants, will play key roles supplying the labor market and then supporting a very large elderly population.

So what will this generation be like when it grows up? In 2003 the Census Bureau made it official that the Latino population had surpassed African Americans to become the nation's largest minority group. Currently, Latinos have many of the characteristics associated with minority group status, such as more poverty and less education than the national average. But will Hispanics be a minority group in the traditional sense 20 or 30 years from now? Or, will they follow the course of other immigrants' offspring, who went through the melting pot experience and emerged into the middle class? Much will depend on how they fare in the schools and then in the workplace. Given their numbers, the whole nation has a stake in the outcome.

Racial, Ethnic Identities Evolve as Nation Changes

BY CHRIS ECHEGARAY
TAMPA TRIBUNE, AUGUST 20, 2006

The labels used to be simple—white, black, Asian, Hispanic and the ubiquitous "other."

But the United States is changing, and so is its racial and ethnic lexicon. With Latinos the largest minority nationwide, labels are more about self-identification and ethnicity, say those who study the trend. The Census Bureau recognized it more than ever in 2000, letting Americans choose two or more racial and ethnic labels for themselves.

The latest census release, 2005 estimates, showed an increase in the Latino population. The estimated Hispanic population is 42.7 million—almost double the 1990 figure. By 2050, it is projected to be 102.6 million—24 percent of the population.

The nation is undergoing a demographic shift, political scientist and Latin American expert Ernesto Sagas said, the expected time for groups to assert their self-identification.

The issue is particularly applicable to Latinos, who are connected by countries of origin and language but not race.

"One of the problems with labels is it's just really a way of organizing the world," said Sagas, a professor at Southern New Hampshire University. "People tend to be very logical and create labels not very representative. One can find an exception to every label."

A Puerto Rican with fair skin, blondish hair and hazel eyes, Aileen Rodriguez remembered filling out forms at a skin cancer screening where she was asked to mark a box describing her race and ethnicity. Rodriguez clicked on the category she identifies with most: white.

"That's me," she said. "I'm white, but I'm white Hispanic. Usually, there's no category like that, so I'll choose Caucasian. I go back and forth. When it comes to identity, it depends on what's the question. I'm bicultural."

Estrella Lopez Clement is in another part of the Hispanic race spectrum—Afro-Cuban. She took exception to the choices on the state's driver license in the 1970s: "white," "black" and "other." She is dark-skinned, but she chose "other." Showing her license to an acquaintance, Clement was stunned.

RACIAL AND ETHNIC TERMS

African-American: Having ancestors from sub-Saharan Africa; black American.

Anglo: A white citizen or inhabitant of the United States who is of non-Hispanic descent.

Asian: Of Asia or its peoples, languages or cultures; a person born or living in Asia, now generally the preferred term.

Black: Any dark-skinned traditional inhabitants of sub-Saharan Africa, Australia or Melanesia or their descendants in other parts of the world.

Hispanic: Spanish or Spanish and Portuguese; usually a Spanish-speaking person of Latin American birth or descent who lives in the United States.

Latin: Designating the languages derived from Latin, the people who speak them, or their countries or cultures; a person whose language is derived from Latin, such as a Spaniard, Italian or Latin American.

Latino: A Latino American; usually a Spanish-speaking person of Latin American birth or descent who lives in the United States.

Spanish: Of Spain or its people, language or culture.

White: A person with a light-colored skin; member of the Caucasoid division of humans.

Source: *Webster's New World College Dictionary*, Fourth Edition

"They looked at the 'O' on the license and said, 'I didn't know you were Oriental.' That was strange," Clement said. "Later, the categories changed, and I chose 'Hispanic.'"

It's the "cosmic race," said the University of South Florida's director of diversity and equal opportunity affairs, Jose Hernandez. "It's a lot of cultures under one rubric. You eventually get to the fact we all are human with certain cultures and heritages. How we define ourselves will continue to change. The conversation will not die."

One part of the conversation is how to distinguish white Hispanics from other whites, commonly called "non-Hispanic whites." The nickname "Anglo" is controversial in some circles, along with the word "Hispanic," because of those words' roots.

In the early 19th century Southwest, Mexicans and the Spanish described the white newcomers from the eastern United States as "Anglos," and it stuck, Sagas said. After the Southwest became part of the United States, Spanish settlers used the word "Hispanic" to differentiate themselves and pale-skinned Mexicans from darker people of mixed ethnicity. It was intended to divide the upper class from the rest, Sagas said.

The census started using the term "Spanish/Hispanic" in 1980. Some railed against the government when the label was introduced, asking for the word "Latino." It's more inclusive, covering people from Latin America, including the indigenous, Hernandez said.

Changes in the 2000 census allowed people to choose "Spanish/Hispanic/Latino," then to identify nationality and race.

In the 2000 census, 98 percent of people chose one race; 2 percent checked two or more.

For the next census in 2010, there is talk of changing the race portion of the questionnaire, but no one is certain what to, census demographer Claudette Bennet said.

A Hybrid Tongue or Slanguage?

BY DANIEL HERNANDEZ
LOS ANGELES TIMES, DECEMBER 27, 2003

On a muggy Sunday afternoon at the Duenas home in South Gate, mariachi music bumped from a boombox on the concrete in the driveway. The roasted smells of carne asada lingered over a folding picnic table, like the easy banter between cousins.

"Le robaron la troca con everything. Los tires, los rines," a visiting cousin said.

Translation: "They robbed the truck with everything. The tires, the rims."

"¿Quieres watermelon?" offered Francisco Duenas, a 26-year-old housing counselor, holding a jug filled with sweet water and watermelon bits.

"Tal vez tiene some of the little tierrita at the bottom."

Translation: "Want watermelon? It might have some of the little dirt at the bottom."

When the Duenas family gathers for weekend barbecues, there are no pauses between jokes and gossip, spoken in English and Spanish. They've been mixing the languages effortlessly, sometimes clumsily, for years, so much so that the back-and-forth is not even noticed.

Spanglish, the fluid vernacular that crosses between English and Spanish, has been a staple in Latino life in California since English-speaking settlers arrived in the 19th century. And for much of that time, it has been dismissed and derided by language purists—"neither good, nor bad, but abominable," as Mexican writer Octavio Paz famously put it.

But the criticism has done little to reduce the prevalence of Spanglish, which today is a bigger part of bilingual life than ever before.

Now it's rapidly moving from Latino neighborhoods into the mainstream. Spanglish is showing up in television and films, with writers using it to bring authenticity to their scripts and to get racy language past network executives. Marketers use it to sell everything from bank accounts to soft drinks. Hallmark now sells Spanglish greeting cards. And McDonald's is rolling out Spanglish TV spots that will air on both Spanish-and English-language networks.

In academia, once a bastion of anti-Spanglish sentiment, the vernacular is now studied in courses with names like "Spanish Phonetics" and "Crossing Borders." Amherst College professor Ilan Stavans published a Spanglish dictionary with hundreds of entries—from gaseteria (which means "gas station") to chaqueta (for "jacket," instead of the Spanish word "saco"). Stavans said new Spanglish words are being created all the time,

> Today, Spanglish is especially popular among young urban Latinos who are U.S.–born.

altering traditional notions of language purity that remained strong just a generation ago.

Growing up, "I was told in school that you shouldn't mix the languages," said Stavans, whose college plans to hold the first Conference of Spanglish in April. "There used to be this approach that if you use a broken tongue, you have a broken tongue. It's not about broken tongues; it's about different tongues, and they are legitimate. I think you're going to see a lot more of that."

The rise of Spanglish says a lot about the demographic shifts in California and other states with large Latino populations.

Migration movements are traditionally accompanied by the mixing of the native language with the newly acquired one. Within a generation or two, the Old Country tongue—whether Polish, Chinese or Italian—usually recedes.

But unlike immigrants from Europe and Asia, Latinos are separated from their cultural homeland, not by vast oceans, but by the border with Mexico and the 90 miles between Cuba and the Florida Keys.

The Latino immigrant population is constantly replenishing itself. Meanwhile, Spanish-language media, such as industry giants Telemundo and Univision, continue to grow, which means that the immigrants' original language remains a force in the community.

Today, Spanglish is especially popular among young urban Latinos who are U.S.–born—people like Francisco Duenas, who was raised in South Gate, lives in Echo Park and works in an office in South Los Angeles. Spanglish, he said, allows him to bridge two cultures: the largely Spanish-speaking world of his parents and the English-language world of work and friends.

"I think this Spanglish, being to go back and forth, it's a way of saying, 'Look, I can do both,'" Duenas said. "And I think here in Los Angeles particularmente, it's not necessary to speak just Spanish or English. No puedes describir la vida aqui [you can't describe life here] without speaking both."

As Spanglish spreads, academics and marketers are finding that it's much more complicated than simply forming sentences with both Spanish and English words.

The most basic part of Spanglish is "code-switching," in which someone inserts or substitutes words from one language into another. For instance, Spanglish might sound like "Vamos a la store para comprar milk." Translation: "Let's go to the store to buy milk."

A more complicated form of Spanglish involves making up words—essentially switching languages within a word itself. It can happen when a word or phrase is translated literally, like perro caliente for

> "It's the schizophrenia of trying to deal with two worlds in one."—San Diego cartoonist Lalo Alcaraz on Spanglish

"hot dog." In other instances, Spanglish is created when an English word is Hispanicized, such as troca or troque for "truck." Speakers might also add the -ear suffix to an English word to make it an improper Spanish verb: parquear, for "to park," for example.

Major regional differences have emerged. In Miami's Little Havana, a Spanglish word for "traitor" is "Kenedito," a reference to exiles' hard feelings over President Kennedy's failed Bay of Pigs invasion. In New York, Puerto Ricans refer to their home on the Lower East Side as "La Loisaida." In some parts of the Southwest, Spanglish speakers say "Ay te watcho" to bid someone farewell.

Just where the sudden popularity of code-switching will end is a matter of debate. Jim Boulet Jr., executive director of English First, a lobbying group opposed to bilingual education, which has railed against Spanglish, thinks the boom is a fleeting trend. He and other critics see Spanglish as a form of slang, not a new language.

"There's always been some form of that," he said. "At one point, it was Yiddish, then the black urban slang, and now Spanglish is the new 'in' thing."

But while academics try to break down Spanglish to understand how it is used, others say it's a code so spontaneous that it's impossible to fully unravel.

It's "a state of mind," said San Diego cartoonist Lalo Alcaraz, whose nationally syndicated strip "La Cucaracha" includes code-switching. "It's the schizophrenia of trying to deal with two worlds in one."

That conflict has set off a debate among Latinos over whether the rise of Spanglish is a good thing.

Patrick Osio Jr., editor of the public affairs website HispanicVista.com, said Spanglish hinders, rather than helps, Latinos' upward mobility.

"A dialectical mixture of the two is not going to get you much anywhere," Osio said. "It may allow you to trade a few barbs with your neighbors and friends, but outside of that, you're doomed."

Indeed, some parents fear their children are too barraged with both languages to adequately learn either.

Veronica Padilla, a 30-year-old mother of two, speaks English with her husband, Spanish with her mother and a mix of both with her children. Freely code-switching herself, Padilla said the results in her children's speech, at least culturally speaking, are appalling.

For instance, her children can't properly name basic Mexican foods.

"A las tortillas les dicen 'tacos,' [they call tortillas 'tacos'] can you believe it? Tacos!" Padilla said while shopping at Latino Factory, a specialty shop, at the Stonewood Shopping Center in Downey.

She shrugged. "That's just the way we talk."

There is perhaps no better place to see how Spanglish is used—and marketed—today than the studios of KJLA-TV, a music programming network that bills itself as the first truly bilingual space on broadcast television for young Latinos.

LATV, as the station is known, broadcasts celebrity interviews as completely bilingual affairs. On a recent show, the hosts asked pop singer Juanes questions in English, and he responded in Spanish. The code-switching at times was fast and furious.

The programming director, Flavio Morales, said the use of Spanglish is purely spontaneous—the way the young people who watch the show actually talk. Morales simply assumes his audience can follow along. And among the 20-something employees at LATV, Spanglish is the norm.

"Hey, welcome back to Mex 2 the Max. ¿Que pasa calabasa?" Morales tells the audience during a music video program. "Check us out at LATV-punto-com, where we have a cool . . . cuarto de chat [chat room]."

Evelyn Casillas, a 19-year-old intern at LATV, said the station's use of two languages reflects the upbringing of both the employees and the studio audiences, which are full of Latino teenagers from all over Los Angeles.

"My parents didn't speak English so a fuerzas aprendi espanol," Casillas said without skipping a beat, explaining how she had been forced to learn Spanish growing up in her Mexican immigrant parents' home in Brea. "My mind just works that way."

"Like the word ansiosa," she added, wringing her hands together. "How can you explain that in English?"

Casillas could translate it as "anxious," but like other Spanglish speakers, she said that sometimes Spanish words just sound better—part of the fun of code-switching.

The bilingual banter has generated interest from advertisers who want to use Spanglish—and the perceived street authenticity that comes with it—to sell their products.

"The advertisers kept saying, 'We want youth, we want Hispanic youth,'" said Yolanda Foster, vice president for marketing of mun2, a Miami-based bilingual music channel similar in format to LATV. The dialogue is mostly English with a Spanish twist—the way she believes many Latino teens speak among themselves.

"They speak English, but they flavor it, or season it, with Spanish terms," Foster said. "Everywhere I go, it's like, 'My God, finally, finally there's something like this.'"

First-generation Latinos roughly between the ages of 14 and 28 represent the fastest-growing youth demographic, according to the U.S. Census Bureau. And an October study by the Pew Hispanic Center in Washington, D.C., found that most second-generation Latinos live in cities and tend to speak both Spanish and English.

"I see it more as a convergence of massive urban youth—it's really an urban youth enchilada," said Tito Zamalloa, a multicultural marketing director at PepsiCo Inc., which recently led a marketing blitz for its Mountain Dew soft drink with the phrase "Toma this!" Toma translates to "drink" or "take."

A new TV advertisement for McDonald's features young and attractive brown-skinned urbanites salivating over Big Macs while a rapper in the background rhymes, "As a matter of fact, te va encantar!" Translation: "You'll love it!"

McDonald's director of U.S. marketing, Max Gallegos, said the ad reflects a shift in the way the company markets itself to Latinos. For years, it produced Spanish-language ads aimed at young Latinos. But because of shifts in demographics, the fast-food giant is focusing more on acculturation with ads that mix references to two cultures.

"It's a big difference . . . embracing the two cultures; that's creating a mind-set of its own," Gallegos said.

And it's not just advertisers who are turning to Spanglish to lend authenticity.

In "Kingpin," an NBC miniseries about a Mexican American drug cartel, the mostly bilingual actors were encouraged to improvise dialogue in some scenes presented entirely in Spanish. David Mills, the show's creator, said the mix of English and Spanish dialogue matched the speaking patterns of the people the characters were based on—giving the program a realistic feel.

On Nickelodeon's popular "Dora the Explorer" cartoon, Dora greets toddler viewers with a cheery "Hola" at the start of each episode and introduces Spanish words throughout the show.

Spanglish—used famously by Arnold Schwarzenegger when he said, "Hasta la vista, baby" in "Terminator 2"—is now showing up in more sustained dialogue in movies like "Real Women Have Curves" and the "Spy Kids" trilogy.

Director James L. Brooks is now filming his next romantic comedy, about a Mexican woman who arrives in Los Angeles looking for love and money. The title: "Spanglish."

Susana Chavez-Silverman, who teaches Spanglish texts in courses at Pomona College and whose memoir about speaking Spanglish during a stay in Argentina will be published next year, said the spread of Spanglish is more than just a linguistic lark.

"This never would've happened 20 years ago, when the idea of multiculturalism wasn't in, the idea of cultural ambiguity wasn't in," she said. "Now it is, and a certain acceptance of Spanglish is a symptom of that."

It's an acceptance that is echoed, more or less, back at the Duenas home, where matriarch Petra Duenas, 63, said the way her family speaks simply shows that the younger ones were raised in an English-speaking world by Spanish-speaking parents. "Since they were little, we taught them Spanish and in school they learned English," she said in Spanish.

Petra Duenas proudly said she didn't mix languages. She has spent decades in Los Angeles, learning some English, but she insisted most of her daily life happens exclusively in Spanish.

But as she explained what her husband does for a living, the reach of Spanglish became clear. Her husband, she said, operates "un troque que arregla los trailers cuando se ponchan en los freeways."

Translation: "A truck that fixes trailers when they break down on freeways."

English Ability by Age, Race and Ethnicity: 2005								
Universe: 2005 Household Population age 5 and over								
	Under 18				18 and over			
	English only	English very well	English less than very well	Total	English only	English very well	English less than very well	Total
Hispanic	3,055,667	4,891,303	1,930,387	9,877,357	5,024,547	9,648,304	12,813,959	27,486,810
Native Born	3,005,527	4,129,264	1,237,132	8,371,923	4,421,801	6,132,020	1,759,426	12,313,247
Foreign Born	50,140	762,039	693,255	1,505,434	602,746	3,516,284	11,054,533	15,173,563
White alone, not Hispanic	29,480,072	1,351,501	399,732	31,231,305	141,242,494	6,064,764	2,855,324	150,162,582
Black alone, not Hispanic	7,303,030	315,036	99,395	7,717,461	22,207,173	1,035,042	560,253	23,802,468
Asian alone, not Hispanic	714,678	941,296	349,772	2,005,746	1,985,827	3,688,101	3,843,809	9,517,737
Other, not Hispanic	1,721,944	226,646	54,545	2,003,135	3,343,527	645,112	293,016	4,281,655
Total	42,275,391	7,725,782	2,833,831	52,835,004	173,803,568	21,081,323	20,366,361	215,251,252
Percent Distribution								
Hispanic	30.9	49.5	19.5	100.0	18.3	35.1	46.6	100.0
Native Born	35.9	49.3	14.8	100.0	35.9	49.8	14.3	100.0
Foreign Born	3.3	50.6	46.1	100.0	4.0	23.2	72.9	100.0
White alone, not Hispanic	94.4	4.3	1.3	100.0	94.1	4.0	1.9	100.0
Black alone, not Hispanic	94.6	4.1	1.3	100.0	93.3	4.3	2.4	100.0
Asian alone, not Hispanic	35.6	46.9	17.4	100.0	20.9	38.7	40.4	100.0
Other, not Hispanic	86.0	11.3	2.7	100.0	78.1	15.1	6.8	100.0
Total	80.0	14.6	5.4	100.0	80.7	9.8	9.5	100.0

Source: Pew Hispanic Center tabulations of 2005 American Community Survey

The Latino Culture Wars

By Seth Kugel
The New York Times, February 24, 2002

In two weeks, Gabriela Minueza, 9, a fourth grader at Public School 95 in Jamaica, Queens, will go to Albany with the school choir for the 25th anniversary conference of the New York State Association for Bilingual Education. She will take the solo in "Preciosa," a patriotic song by the Puerto Rican writer Rafael Hernandez that was recently recorded by the Puerto Rican singer Marc Anthony. At one point, she will step forward and sing in Spanish:

> Whatever happens
> I will be Puerto Rican
> I will be Puerto Rican
> Wherever I go
> Because it's in my blood
> Inherited from my parents, and proudly I repeat
> I love you Puerto Rico!

But whatever happens and wherever she goes, Gabriela will never be Puerto Rican. She is Guatemalan, born here to immigrant parents, and with traces of Mayan features to prove it. The classmates who will sing behind her, few of them Puerto Rican either, mistake her for Chinese, if anything.

But in the sphere of New York elementary school music, as in language, culture and politics, being Latino in New York is tied to being Caribbean in general and Puerto Rican in particular.

New York has the world's most diverse Spanish-speaking population, but it is still a city in which the Latino cultural icons are people like the Puerto Rican pop star Jennifer Lopez and the Boston Red Sox slugger (and pride of Washington Heights) Manny Ramirez. The city gave birth to the Nuyorican Poets Cafe, and is a place where the Puerto Rican street toughs of "West Side Story" and the romantic Latino aura of Spanish Harlem still resonate. A city in which the biggest Latino parades celebrate Puerto Rican and Dominican pride. A city of salsa and merengue.

So, even as Mexicans, Ecuadoreans and others come to the city in increasing numbers, Puerto Ricans and Dominicans still make up the biggest pieces of the Latino pie. Of New York's 2.2 million Latinos, 830,000 are Puerto Rican and 579,000 Dominican, placing them first and second in a growing population, up from 1.7 million in 1990. That means Mexican, Central American and South American immigrants and their children not only have to adjust to the broader American culture, they try to avoid being engulfed by the dominant Latino culture.

On any cultural battlefield, the first skirmish usually involves language. Just about every Spanish speaker in the city, regardless of age, feels a Caribbean breeze in their Spanish. To most Latin Americans, a bean is a frijol, but for Caribbeans, and thus in New York, it is an habichuela. And though many South Americans find the Caribbean word for bus, guagua, ridiculous, some say it occasionally escapes from their lips.

Clara Bosworth, who lives in East Harlem, arrived in New York from Ecuador 38 years ago, in her late 20's. At first she suffered, grappling with a tongue both familiar yet strange. Eventually, she took to calling beans habichuelas, and has been known to say "guagua." She even breaks out with the Puerto Rican exclamation "Ay bendito!" and the occasional "OH-oh," the Dominican expression of surprise that starts with a high-pitched "OH" and flows into the lower-pitched "oh."

> ## On any cultural battlefield, the first skirmish usually involves language.

Like about every other South American immigrant, she has a "bicho" story. In a Spanish-English dictionary, bicho means bug or insect. But in much of the Caribbean it is a vulgarity that refers to part of the male anatomy. Soon after her arrival in New York, Ms. Bosworth was at a party. A friend pointed to her wrist, which was red. "What happened to you, Blanca?" he asked.

"Oh, I don't know when," she said, in Spanish. "But this bicho bit me."

Another man overheard and chastised her: "Look, Senora, you need to learn how to speak!"

"I turned red as a tomato," she said. As she fled the party, she realized that not only would she have to learn English, she would have to relearn Spanish.

Puerto Rico: Still Dominant

Puerto Rican culture has long been the city's dominant Latino culture. Even so, the Puerto Rican population has declined to 38 percent today from 80 percent of Latinos in 1960, according to the Lewis Mumford Center for Urban and Regional Research at SUNY-Albany, based on adjusted 2000 census figures. But because the Puerto Ricans were here first, learned English first, opened restaurants first, fought for their rights first and ran for office first, they still wield an influence that exceeds their shrinking demographic share.

"Puerto Rico was the original common denominator," said Juan Flores, a professor in the department of black and Puerto Rican studies at Hunter College.

But even as the proportion of Puerto Ricans shrank, many of their replacements came from the Dominican Republic. Inter-island rivalries make some people reluctant to admit it, but the two cultures have many similarities, from the food they eat to the music they make to the Spanish they speak to the baseball they play to the African blood in their veins. Add in a few Cubans, and the Hispanic Caribbean accounts for 67 percent of Latinos in New York; the rest are almost evenly divided between Mexico/Central America and South America, at about 16 percent each.

The neighborhoods in which Latino groups live reinforce the Caribbean dominance. There are almost 200 census tracts in the city where Caribbean Hispanics make up more than 50 percent of the overall population, but there are no such tracts for either Mexicans and Central Americans combined or for South Americans, data from the Mumford Center show.

That pressures the non-Caribbean groups, especially students. They are jockeying to maintain their own identity, while taking on Caribbean traits as they try to ease into American culture.

"Young Latinos from different groups will tend to gravitate to Puerto Ricans," Mr. Flores said, "because Puerto Ricans have been around, they know the ropes, they know the way of walking and talking, rather than being fresh off the boat, being greenhorns."

Younger Latinos also look to Dominican culture. Luis Delgado, 15, a freshman at Manhattan Academy for Science and Mathematics, lives in Washington Heights, which is so heavily Dominican that it elected the first Dominican, Guillermo Linares, to the City Council in 1991. Luis's Spanish accent is pure Dominican, and he is scolded by his Ecuadorean parents when he uses the informal Dominican "Que?" for "What?" instead of the more formal "Mande?"

"It's not like you do it on purpose," Luis said of his cultural makeover. "It just slips out."

But essentially, Luis's friends say, he has become Dominican. Though he eats ceviche, an Ecuadorean fish salad, at home, he is happiest with the combination of rice, beans and meat known as "the Dominican flag."

"He knows how to talk Dominican," said Laiheng Cabral, a Dominican classmate. "He knows how to dance Dominican."

The Caribbean Gatekeepers

Latinos from the Caribbean carry the day politically, too. There are 24 Hispanic elected officials representing New York on the local, state and federal level, according to Angelo Falcon, the senior policy executive for the Puerto Rican Legal Defense and Education Fund. Of them, 21 are Puerto Rican, 3 Dominican. So it's not surprising that the city's best-known Latino politicians, like Herman Badillo (the first Puerto Rican to hold a boroughwide office), Fernando Ferrer (the former Bronx borough president) and Mr. Linares (the former Council member and currently a deputy public advocate) are part of that lineage.

Citizenship by birth has given Puerto Ricans enduring political power, even as their numbers decline.

"One of the things people need to understand is that while the demographics are very diverse, in terms of the Latino electorate it's not a straight translation," Mr. Falcon said. "Puerto Ricans may be 36 percent of the Latino population, but may be 60 to 70 percent of Latinos who vote." Dominicans' history of political activism, he added, and their "hypersegregation" in Upper Manhattan have helped them take some power, too.

"The reality is, they are the same, and they are not the same," Mr. Ferrer said, referring to Latino groups. "It depends on the moment, the issue and the venue."

Mr. Falcon said, "Puerto Ricans and Dominicans wind up being gatekeepers, so other groups have to deal with them."

A Puerto Rican Boyfriend

Many embrace the majority culture.

Sandra Moya grew up in Woodside, Queens, and went to high school in her parents' native Ecuador. She became interested in Puerto Rico only after she entered La Guardia Community College in 1986.

"A lot of Ecuadoreans resent that I'm more Puerto Rican than Ecuadorean," said Ms. Moya, who is now director of the Leonard Covello Senior Center in East Harlem, which is heavily Puerto Rican.

When she was 19, Ms. Moya brought home a Puerto Rican boyfriend. She said her mother's reaction was something like, "Jesus, Lord have mercy!" Since then, Ms. Moya has tortured her with a string of Puerto Rican boyfriends, including three fiances. One mother taught her to cook, so now she makes Puerto Rican food like arroz con gandules (rice with pigeon peas) much more often than Ecuadorean dishes. When her brother married a Cuban, her mother said she had been cursed by the Caribbean.

A few years ago, Ms. Moya got the ultimate stamp of approval for her Puerto Rican status. She appeared in a picture of future leaders in the publication "Puerto Rican Women Achievers in N.Y.C."

There are 144,000 Ecuadoreans in New York, making them the city's fourth-largest Latino group after the Mexicans (196,000). They find comfort in Ecuadorean organizations, grocery stores and dozens of restaurants. But fitting in is not easy for everyone.

Michelle Morazan, 26, is one of the fewer than 10,000 Nicaraguans in the city. But since arriving at 3, her life has been braided with the Caribbean. Her mother married a Dominican and her grandmother a Puerto Rican. Ms. Morazan lived in the Dominican Republic briefly, but now lives in Upper Manhattan and has no Nicaraguan friends in New York; not on purpose, but because there are so few around.

"In many ways I probably identify more with Dominicans than with Nicaraguans," she said. "We feel left out; we need to associate with something. I have to remind myself that I'm Nicaraguan. I hate to say that. It seems terrible."

Waiting for Their Moment

Still, among non-Caribbean Latinos, there is no set response to their minority role. Some resist the dominant Puerto Rican and Dominican cultures, some shrug in acceptance, some don't even realize they're being absorbed, and a few are waiting for their moment to take center stage.

Marizol Minueza, the mother of Gabriela, the fourth-grade singer, isn't too worried about her daughter's singing a Puerto Rican anthem. Ms. Minueza, who came from Guatemala at 18, had misgivings at first, but felt better when the music teacher told her the performance would deepen her daughter's multicultural education.

Gabriela's parents have also felt the Caribbean influence in their lives.

"You no longer speak Guatemalan, you speak Puerto Rican," Ms. Minueza's mother scolds her. Gabriela's father, Gober, who came to New York at 6, said his father expunged Puerto Rican words from his Spanish.

"When we brought different words home, he would be on top of us not to say those words," Mr. Minueza said. "Guatemalans have this thing that Puerto Ricans eat a lot of the letters, that was mostly his concern."

What of Gabriela? Her solo is a Puerto Rican song, but P.S. 95, has festivals celebrating the diversity of its pupils, who are from Latin America and Asia. Last October, during a celebration of multiculturalism, she proudly showed off an embroidered rainbow of a dress from Guatemala.

Hispanics Have Made Great Strides But Are Still Striving

BY SARAH COPPOLA
AUSTIN AMERICAN-STATESMAN, NOVEMBER 20, 2003

When Robert Carlin attended Round Rock Elementary School in the early 1950s, he felt frightened as one of the few Hispanic students there.

"If you spoke Spanish, you were punished by not being allowed to go to recess," Carlin said. "The other kids wouldn't choose you for certain games because you couldn't communicate."

Today, after earning bachelor's and master's degrees, Carlin is principal of that same school where he once felt afraid. Renamed Berkman Elementary, the campus is now a bilingual school where some classes are taught in both Spanish and English; Latino students there are given special attention to ensure they'll succeed.

"We've learned a lot," Carlin said. "There were no such programs when I was a child."

Carlin is one of an estimated 51,000 Latinos who make Williamson County their home. Early last century, Hispanics migrated to towns such as Taylor to farm and raise families. Many of them stayed. Williamson has more native-born, second- and third-generation families than other counties statewide. Latinos, now 17 percent of the county's population, are moving here for other reasons today: to work for large companies such as Dell Inc. or to build this growing county's roads and homes. Latinos here are better educated and earn larger incomes than Latinos statewide.

Even as Hispanics emerge as a force in Williamson, they continue to struggle in some ways. In every school district, fewer Latino students passed state achievement tests than their white peers. Nearly half of the families in Williamson's indigent health care program are Latino. One-third of the prison population is Latino. And only a few Hispanics occupy elected leadership positions.

Some Latino immigrants and their children are having trouble fitting in simply because they don't speak English; many schools and police agencies here have only a handful of Spanish-speaking employees.

For the Hispanic community, some of the old ways are fading, too; Hispanic households are less likely to speak Spanish than the typical Hispanic family in Texas. Still, all around the county, Latino cul-

Article by Sarah Coppola from the *Austin American-Statesman*, November 30, 2003. Copyright © *Austin American-Statesman*. Reprinted with permission.

ture is alive. On Saturday night, Hispanics crowd El Vaquero dance club to do the cumbia. Joe Madrigal runs the local chapter of the National Hispanic Institute and coaches Latino youths in public debate. Saul Garcia painted his Round Rock home bright green, a nod to Mexicans' belief that color signifies vibrancy. They are the faces of Hispanics in Williamson County.

Education

Julio Cruz moved from Veracruz, Mexico, in August. The Georgetown High School student doesn't speak English and is often baffled in class. He wants to succeed. But he lacks the words he needs to ask his teachers questions. Putting aside an English-only textbook in his English as a Second Language class, Cruz shook his head and sighed. "I feel like a stranger," he said in Spanish. "I want to communicate, but I can't."

Statistics show that Latino students here, particularly those who can't speak English, are lagging behind their peers. Roughly a quarter of the county's students are Hispanic; 5 percent are enrolled in English as a Second Language classes.

In 2003, Hispanic students from three out of 10 school districts (Thrall, Taylor and Jarrell) scored lower than the average statewide Hispanic passing rate—60 percent—on state achievement tests. Latinos in the Leander school district scored highest: 73 percent passing.

School districts are slowly finding ways to improve those scores. Round Rock, for example, hired Mary Villarreal as principal of one of its four bilingual schools, Bluebonnet Elementary. Villareal started a mentoring program at the school and tested students throughout the year to track their progress. The results were impressive: 93 percent of Bluebonnet's Latino students passed the fourth-grade English writing test in 2003, up from only 47 percent the year before.

Core subjects such as math and science are taught in Spanish at Bluebonnet. The school has two bilingual teachers for each grade from pre-kindergarten through third and one each for fourth- and fifth-graders.

Leander schools offer bilingual education at two elementary campuses and bus other Spanish-speaking students there. That district also provides an evening English-proficiency class for Hispanic parents.

Middle schools and high schools are trying to make do with limited bilingual staffs. At Georgetown High School, for example, one bilingual teacher's aide moves from class to class, and student volunteers from Southwestern University also help Spanish-speaking students translate their work.

Teacher Craig Boneau groups together Spanish-speaking students with bilingual students. He also modifies assignments, such as providing Spanish-only students with more vocabulary work. Boneau, who doesn't speak Spanish, has trouble conveying ideas to those students.

"It's a problem," said Boneau, a third-year biology teacher, recalling a former student who was very bright and would have "easily been an A student" if not for a language barrier.

Experts say attempts to fix the problem often fall short because districts don't have the money or resources to keep pace with a wave of new immigrants.

"They're having to absorb and educate large numbers of kids who are coming from (disadvantaged) circumstances," said Jose Limon, director of the Center for Mexican American Studies at the University of Texas.

Edna Aguirre Rehbein, 48, once struggled as a Spanish-speaking student in San Antonio; now, she is executive director of the Round Rock Higher Education Center. Historically, she said, many Latino students have started working after graduating from high school, to help their families, instead of attending college. Rehbein hopes to change that: When the center opens a new Texas State University campus in 2005, Rehbein projects that 15 percent—or about 525—of its 3,500 students will be Latino.

"It's a myth that Hispanics don't value education," she said.

> "There's still a lot of people who perceive (Latinos) in a certain way and stereotype us."—
> Jaime Alaniz, State Farm Insurance

Business

Pepe Arteaga has been back and forth to Mexico four times in the past two months.

First, he drives to Laredo to collect the pewter frames and flatware that his family designed and cast at its factory in San Miguel de Allende, Guanajuato. Then Arteaga loads the pieces in his green pickup, brings them back and displays them in his small shop on the Georgetown square.

"I did my research," said Arteaga, who recently moved from Mexico to Round Rock. "It's a good place for specialty stores. I like the small-town feel, and the people are very friendly. It reminds me a little of San Miguel."

Arteaga is one of thousands of Latinos who have moved to Williamson County to work. Census figures show that Latino households here on average earn $51,000; white households earn $62,000.

More Hispanics here work in management or professional jobs (26 percent) than Hispanics statewide (18 percent). Jaime Alaniz is an automation supervisor with State Farm Insurance who moved to Round Rock in 1980. Alaniz and his wife are planning to adopt a child, and they've chosen to live and work here largely because of the area's safe neighborhoods and good schools, he said.

"There's still a lot of people who perceive (Latinos) in a certain way and stereotype us," Alaniz said. "They fail to realize that a lot of us are professionals. We believe in ourselves and in helping our children become future leaders."

Dell, the county's largest employer, recruits at Hispanic universities and has a social networking group for Latino employees.

At the same time, some Williamson County Hispanics have looked to Austin for better paying jobs. The grandparents of Jesse Ancira Jr. migrated to Taylor in the early 1900s to pick cotton. Ancira still lives in Taylor but works in Austin as general counsel for Texas Comptroller Carole Keeton Strayhorn.

"Over half of my peers in school moved away," said Ancira, who graduated from Taylor High School in 1982. "In this part of the county, unless you are in one of the local government positions or own a business, there are few professional openings for anyone."

The need to build roads, homes and businesses has brought a fresh wave of low-wage and undocumented workers to Williamson. One in five Hispanic men here have industrial or transportation jobs; a quarter work in construction or maintenance, according to the 2000 U.S. census.

"You go to any construction site in America and look at who's pouring the cement, who's putting on the roofs, who's doing the frames; you're going to see a large number of Hispanics," said Steve Murdock, a state demographer based at Texas A&M University. "Hispanics today are the Irish 200 years ago."

Construction worker Arturo Banda lives in Austin but said he works in Williamson because the builders pay better.

"In Austin, it's too cheap," he said during a break from driving a forklift in a new neighborhood near Dell Diamond. "This is where you make the money."

Each month Banda sends a fifth of his paycheck to his mother in Mexico. Nationally, immigrant workers send $14.5 billion of their earnings to relatives in Mexico each year, statistics show. Said J.R. Gonzales, chairman of the U.S. Hispanic Chamber of Commerce, "Their country is dependent on ours, but we're just as dependent on them, particularly in Williamson, where you have a lot of growth."

Police and Courts

Defense lawyer Will Aguilar knew his client, a Latino man, was innocent. The man had been wrongly accused of molesting a girl; he'd been hanging out with friends at the time. But Aguilar had trouble finding the man's acquaintances to vouch for him.

"Many Latinos go to work and go home; they don't spend a lot of time driving around; they might not know specific locations or phone numbers," Aguilar said. "Some also don't stay in one place very long. So it can be difficult to find witnesses."

Spanish-speaking defendants have an especially tough time in the justice system, defense lawyers said. They are often more deferential to prosecutors and may settle for harsher pleas. If their testimony needs to be interpreted in court, the confusion can distract and annoy a jury. And undocumented Latinos are often reluctant to testify as witnesses.

Skin color can be another factor. "Juries in Williamson tend to be older, less transient and Caucasian," said defense lawyer Richard Segura, who has practiced in Williamson and Travis counties. "It's a tougher seller when a defense attorney is representing a black or Hispanic there than in Travis."

Latinos make up 30 percent of the adults arrested in Williamson. Thirty percent of Williamson County offenders in the state prison system are Hispanic.

Language barriers can also slightly skew arrest rates; officers may be more apt to arrest a Hispanic if the officer cannot understand that person, said Larry Hoover, director of the Police Research Center at Sam Houston State University.

Very few police officers in this county are bilingual: five out of 54

"With the Latino community, you see all the time that they're afraid to talk to police, especially if an officer can't speak Spanish."—Jesse Rodriguez, Cedar Park, TX, police officer

---

officers in Cedar Park, for example; six out of 47 in Georgetown. Though police agencies aren't doing much to recruit more Spanish speakers, they have tried other approaches to deal with the shortage: spreading out bilingual officers over shifts or borrowing bilingual officers from nearby agencies. Sheriff's deputies can dial a language line that patches through a Spanish translator.

Only one police department in this county, Round Rock, offers extra pay to officers fluent in Spanish.

Capt. Chris Bratton started a program four years ago that offers Spanish lessons to Round Rock officers; 18 of that agency's 116 officers now speak Spanish. The program pairs officers with Hispanic mentors from outside the police force.

"We sit down and translate different situations or write a script—maybe how to stop someone to do a search or talk to someone who'd been driving erratically," mentor Guillermo Calderon said.

A subtler problem—and one that's tougher to solve, officers said—is the apprehension some Hispanics feel about police. Latino immigrants, in particular, may come from countries where the police were cruel and corrupt; undocumented workers may hesitate to report crimes for fear of being deported.

"With the Latino community, you see all the time that they're afraid to talk to police, especially if an officer can't speak Spanish," bilingual officer Jesse Rodriguez of Cedar Park said. "I always sense a feeling of ease on their part once I start communicating in Spanish."

Health Care

Signs at the door of the Round Rock Health Clinic greet patients in two languages: "Round Rock Health Clinic" and "Clinica de la Familia."

On a recent morning, Leander residents Rene and Alin Juarez brought their 2-year-old son, Samuel, to the clinic. Samuel, who qualified for the state's Children's Health Insurance Plan, had a cough. Rene Juarez works at a restaurant that offers heath insurance, but he cannot afford it, he said.

"It's hard because most insurance is very expensive," Rene said in Spanish. "Where I work, I only know one person who has insurance." So when Rene and Alin get sick, they usually tough it out with over-the-counter medicines.

Many Hispanics in Williamson County are struggling to get health care even though this county is one of the most affluent in the state. Latinos make up 40 percent of the people enrolled in the county's indigent health care program and 80 percent of those enrolled in the primary health care program, which serves the working poor. Though Williamson does not track uninsured residents by ethnicity, 59 percent of Latinos in Texas are uninsured.

Like the Juarez family, many uninsured Latinos seek help at the county's four public health clinics in Cedar Park, Georgetown, Round Rock and Taylor. Some health care workers, such as Dr. Jane Shepherd of the Georgetown Community Clinic, are trying to learn Spanish to keep up.

"We have to be able to speak it, not just have a translator available," Shepherd said. That clinic sees 1,100 patients a month; 40 percent are Latino and a quarter of them speak Spanish only.

The large number of Latinos seeking health care is because of low-paying jobs, language and cultural barriers and transportation problems, health experts said. Latinos who don't speak English, for example, may have difficulty interviewing for a job with health insurance. Funding cuts imposed during the last state legislative session also have hurt.

Illegal immigrants in particular can be reluctant to seek care. Health care workers said they're trying to change that mentality. Andy Martinez, chief executive officer of the Round Rock Health Clinic, distributes pamphlets at schools and churches notifying Hispanics of the clinic's services. "It is not our job to catch folks breaking the law," Martinez said. "Our primary focus is to care for the community."

The House That Used to Be in Mexico

By Felix F. Gutierrez
Los Angeles Times, January 11, 2004

Up the street and around the corner from my family home in South Pasadena is a single-story adobe with red roof tiles and a cactus garden. When I was a boy, El Adobe Flores seemed an outdated relic. But what happened there on Jan. 11, 1847, greatly affected my ancestors, me and my children. What we learned can also benefit all Californians.

One hundred fifty-seven years ago, Californios under Mexican officer Jose Maria Flores met in the adobe on the Rancho Rincon de San Pascual to discuss making peace with invading U.S. forces. Eight months earlier, the U.S. had declared war on Mexico and claimed California, then part of Mexico, as its own. Mexican troops had moved south, seizing many weapons as they went.

But the pobladores, or settlers, of Los Angeles rose up in September 1846, pushing the U.S. occupiers onto ships anchored at San Pedro. Using pistols, lances, lassoes and superior horsemanship, the Californios enjoyed "a long winning streak, from late September to mid-December, capturing the Americans at Chino . . . defeating the Navy at San Pedro . . . and exacting a grim toll at San Pasqual and La Natividad," according to historian Neal Harlow.

In December, 600 U.S. troops regrouped in San Diego and moved north. Ahead of them lay Flores' homeland defense force of 500 Californio militia members and volunteers. Their "courageous determination to defend and preserve their nationality offset the disparity of weapons, munitions and numbers of soldiers," wrote historian Antonio Maria Osio in 1851. But the Californios were outgunned in battles by the San Gabriel River and at La Mesa. On Jan. 10, the U.S. reoccupied Los Angeles.

The next day, the Californios met in the adobe to assess their options, which included a peace offer from Lt. Col. John C. Fremont. (El Adobe Flores honors Jose Maria Flores, the Californios' last Mexican commander, who continued fighting in the south.)

On Jan. 12, Andres Pico's "Californian Forces under the Mexican Flag" met Fremont's commissioners in the home of Don Tomas Feliz. The following day, they signed the Treaty of Cahuenga, which promised "equal rights and privileges . . . to every citizen of California as are enjoyed by the citizens of the United States of North America." But this and similar provisions in the Treaty of Guadalupe Hidalgo, which ended the U.S.–Mexican War about a year later, were not respected. Californios were subjected to a conqueror's unequal justice, lynchings, land frauds and other abuses well into the last half of the 19th century.

> We didn't come to the United States. The United States came to us via its Army, Navy and Marines.

El Adobe Flores is more than a historical footnote to me. My ancestors were among the Californios who fought invading U.S. forces.

Like many Latinos, my presence in the United States is the result of America's self-proclaimed Manifest Destiny. We didn't come to the United States. The United States came to us via its Army, Navy and Marines. Its territorial expansion into Latin America swallowed up us as well as land.

My father once told me without anger, "The Anglos came. We welcomed them. Then they turned against us." Others said, "We didn't cross the border. The border crossed us." Though Mexicans caught in the U.S. expansion could relocate to Mexico—across the new border—my ancestors had no Mexico to go back to. Like most, they stayed put. And we're still here.

My great-grandfather headed north for gold in 1848, made a fortune, then lost it when the 49ers arrived. Later, a blacksmith in El Monte, he repaired covered wagons and shoed Union Army horses during the Civil War. Friends included Californios and Anglos whose surnames now grace Southern California cities: Pio Pico, Bernardo Yorba and Juan Temple.

Baptized at the San Gabriel Mission in the 1870s, my grandfather became a cement contractor, laying irrigation ditches and sidewalks as agriculture and housing boomed. He played baseball for the Monrovia Merchants and was a deputy sheriff in Arcadia.

Born in 1918, my father entered school speaking only Spanish. He grew up in a "polyglot neighborhood of many paisanos, Negroes, a few Italians, Jews, Spaniards, Americans and a Japanese family" in Monrovia, where he endured the "segregations imposed upon Mexicans, Negroes and Filipinos." Adopting an "I'll show 'em" attitude, he went to college and became a teacher.

Although adapting to an Anglos' world and offering to share our ways with them, my forebears discovered that many newcomers believed the only meaningful remnants of Mexican California were the colorful names of mountains, rivers and towns. They felt we could learn more from them than they from us. And learn we did. My family absorbed both sides, learning the language and ways of Anglos without rejecting its own culture and language.

I grew up and still live in a multiracial, multilingual and multicultural world. I live in what used to be Mexico. Nearby is a Mexico whose people cross borders and live on multicultural borderlands. My Mexican-born mother grew up and graduated from college in the U.S. Though proudly a naturalized U.S. citizen, she told her children about Mexico and the importance of maintaining its values while learning from people of all races.

Living in East Los Angeles through the mid-1950s, my parents had many Anglo friends. But our world was bigger than brown and white. My father's best boyhood friend spent World War II behind barbed wire with other Japanese Americans. My mother's closest teaching colleague was African American. We spent time in both their homes.

Latinos today are reshaping the United States' Manifest Destiny. Though many are immigrants, we don't fit into the "forget-your-past" melting pot. Our prototype for America's future is a stew pot in which people retain their identities while contributing to and absorbing the flavors of others.

Though many are dark-skinned, we are not clones of a nation that once viewed race in only black and white. At more than 38 million people and growing, Latinos in America can be white, brown, black and Asian Pacific. We can be Catholics, Protestants, Jews and Muslims and still be full-blooded Latinos.

African Americans, Asian Pacific Americans, Latinos and Native Americans already make up the majority of Californians and are projected to become the nation's majority by midcentury. As they and their multiracial children increase, all Americans will need to find ways to live in a world of more than one language, culture and race. Latinos have been doing this for generations. Others might help themselves by taking a closer look at how we've done it.

Changes in Rhythm for Florida

By John-Thor Dahlburg
Los Angeles Times, June 28, 2004

The gaudy plastic palms blaze with light, speakers boom the cucu bop, cucu bop rhythm of salsa—and the floor at the Goldcoast Ballroom quickly fills.

A Mexican American relocating from Chicago for her sales job swivels on the gleaming hardwood with a Peruvian student. A long-haired paparazzo from Ecuador whirls beside a woman from the Dominican Republic. Elegantly turned out in a slate-gray suit, and making catlike moves, there is one of the legends of Latin dance: Pedro Aguilar, 77, known as "Cuban Pete."

Despite his nickname, Cuban Pete is Puerto Rican, raised in the barrios of New York. Perhaps the most celebrated mambo dancer of all time, he moved to the Miami area in 1982, and has been witness to the large-scale arrival of New Latins.

"It's not just Cubans in Florida anymore," Aguilar says. "It's people from all over Latin America."

In a major demographic shift with implications for politics as well as the humdrum minutiae of life—including the use of parks and the kinds of foods sold in supermarkets—Florida's Latinos, more than 2.6 million strong and growing each day, are undergoing a metamorphosis. Cubans and Cuban Americans, long the majority in the state, have been reduced in the last decade to a distinct if still dominant minority.

What's more, in large part due to the newcomers, people of Spanish language and heritage are no longer concentrated in a few locations like Miami's Little Havana, settled by refugees fleeing Fidel Castro's Cuba, or the older cigar-rolling Cuban district of Ybor City in Tampa.

There is now a Little Caracas of Venezuelans in the Miami suburb of Doral, a Colombian enclave in the Broward County city of Weston, and pockets of Guatemalans in Lake Worth near Palm Beach.

In rural inland towns like Immokalee and Sebring, food markets with names like Azteca cater to Mexican farmworkers and sell votive candles with the image of the Virgin of Guadalupe, Mexico's patron saint. In formerly Anglo suburbs of Fort Lauderdale, gas stations offer hot Argentine beef turnovers.

For the mayor of Orlando, Florida's sixth-largest city, the most significant trend in his area is the surge in Latinos, chiefly Puerto Ricans.

"We now have about 400,000 Hispanic residents in central Florida," said Buddy Dyer, a Democrat.

Even in Miami and environs, long labeled Havana North, the ethnic mix has been transformed. There are so many newcomers from South America and Caribbean islands other than Cuba that in the last three years the Miami-Dade County Parks Service has built 26 soccer fields and plans at least 23 more. (Cubans traditionally prefer baseball.)

To meet the needs of a changing readership, the county public libraries have bought cookbooks from Venezuela, Mexico, Nicaragua and other Latin countries, including works by a celebrated Argentine cook, the late Dona Petrona C. de Gandulfo.

One of the sharpest differences between Florida and California is the extraordinary variety of the Latino population, says Dario Moreno, professor of political science at Florida International University. In California, an overwhelming 77% of Latinos are Mexican or Mexican American. In Florida, people of Cuban birth or descent constitute the largest group, but these days, only about a third of the whole.

"Just because you speak Spanish, no one assumes you're Cuban anymore," Moreno said.

Nearly half a million Puerto Ricans make up 18% of Florida Latinos, Mexicans another 13%. The 2000 census found close to 1 million Floridians with other Latino roots—including Colombians, Venezuelans, Dominicans, Nicaraguans and Argentines.

Some of Florida's New Latins are poor, illiterate or in the United States illegally. Many, though, are entrepreneurs or professionals, in contrast with most of the Latino immigration to California.

"Whatever country you talk about, with the exception of the Mariel boatlift [from Cuba], it's the middle and upper class," said John T. Gaubatz, a law professor at the University of Miami. "Just pick your Latin American country, and if things get dicey, there'll be another wave of successful and well-off people to Florida."

Because of Argentina's economic collapse, Colombia's ongoing guerrilla war, Venezuela's political turmoil and the woes of other nations in the Southern Hemisphere, there are countless new Dairy Queen franchisees, restaurateurs and business owners now in the Sunshine State.

New Latins have injected new life into the places they have settled. One seven-block strip of Collins Avenue in Miami Beach was suffering from the exodus of Jewish retirees but has been revitalized by new businesses representing half a dozen South American nations, including a Brazilian martial arts studio, a Peruvian seafood restaurant and an Argentine grocery.

Last year, economic opportunity lured Ramon Ojeda from Venezuela. Ojeda has an MBA from Penn State and worked eight years in his home country for Cargill, the U.S. agribusiness giant. He was offered a job in Peru. Instead, he came to Orlando, where he is president of the area's Hispanic Chamber of Commerce.

"I am living proof that central Florida is the right place to be for Hispanics," said Ojeda, who is married with two children. "The community is wonderful, it's growing, it's challenging. And we'll continue to see more and more Hispanic migration."

Some better-off Latinos come to Florida temporarily to attend university, spend the austral summer in a second home or are otherwise in transit. Some long-term residents, driven from their homelands by warfare or political and economic upheaval, dream of going back someday.

"We leave the country, but we do not close the door," said Fernando Larrea, a Peruvian who moved to Florida 15 years ago and manages an Argentine-style restaurant in the Orlando suburb

---

"We leave the country, but we do not close the door."—Fernando Larrea, a Peruvian living in Florida

---

of Casselberry. Larrea and his wife still have not decided whether to apply for U.S. citizenship. The two oldest of their three children, who have graduated from college, have become citizens.

*****

The Puerto Ricans, as U.S. citizens, have a unique story. In the 1980s, builders from the Orlando area set up sales offices in Puerto Rico to market entire tracts of new homes in central Florida, where some properties cost only half as much as on the densely populated island. Disney World also was hiring. Puerto Ricans came by the planeloads.

"At that time, there weren't many bilingual Americans who were willing to take on service jobs," recalled Elizabeth Mariaca, who owned a real estate agency in San Juan for more than 20 years and now lives in the upscale South Florida town of Wellington. "Disney got bilingual employees who were citizens."

Like Cuban Pete, many Puerto Ricans have been relocating from the New York area for the same reasons other Americans come to Florida: sunshine, economic opportunity, a nice place to retire. About three months ago, in a strip mall outside the rural city of Lakeland, Manuel Fuentes opened a hair salon and gift shop with a fellow New York–born Puerto Rican.

"I moved to Florida because it's a lot calmer, a lot cleaner, and I'm ready for a slower pace," said Fuentes, 49. "Here we have a good chance to build, to start a successful business."

Even in the southern part of the state, Cubans are now outnumbered. In Miami-Dade and neighboring Monroe and Broward counties, Cubans and Cuban Americans account for 43% of Latinos, according to Synovate Diversity, a research company that tracks trends in major U.S. Latino markets.

Every Sunday, the complex cocktail of Hispanidad Florida style goes on display under the twirling, mirrored ball at the Goldcoast, located in an otherwise drab shopping center in Coconut Creek, a bedroom suburb of Fort Lauderdale. For a $10 entry fee, men and women can sway and slink for three hours to salsa, mambo, merengue and other Latin dance music.

Surrounded by friends and fans, and squiring dance partner Barbara Craddock, Cuban Pete celebrated his 77th birthday at the ballroom this month. Other regulars come to chat and mingle with Spanish speakers like themselves.

"It's becoming a meeting place for the local Hispanic population,"

What makes the New Latins such an alluring prize for political strategists is the fact their party loyalties have not yet gelled.

---

said Judith E. Crocker, a Venezuelan immigrant. She publishes a Spanish-language monthly newspaper, En USA, that marked its second anniversary this month. Crocker is her own one-woman staff, writing articles, shooting photographs and signing up advertisers, but she is convinced she has struck gold: a potential readership of more than 250,000 Latinos who live in the greater Fort Lauderdale area.

"The market is so big here," Crocker said.

*****

In a state where a little more than 500 votes decided the outcome of the last presidential election, the fast-paced growth of Florida's Latino population is being carefully charted by Republicans and Democrats, who hope to ride the trend to victory in November.

What makes the New Latins such an alluring prize for political strategists is the fact their party loyalties have not yet gelled.

"The Cubans are, because of Cuba, staunch Republicans," said Democratic state Rep. Christopher L. Smith of Fort Lauderdale, who is in charge of his party's efforts to elect more legislators in 2004. "The non-Cuban Hispanics are swing voters. This is the population you have to work for."

Politically, however, the longer established Cuban community still rules. Of the more than 1 million registered Latino voters in Florida, as many as half may still be Cuban American. All three Latinos in the state Senate are Cuban American; of the 14 members of the Hispanic Caucus in Florida's House of Representatives, 11 are Cuban American, one Puerto Rican, one Mexican American and one Colombian American. The three Florida Latinos in the U.S. House of Representatives are Cuban Americans.

Slowly, though, a trans-Latino identity is taking root. Nowadays, even a venerable temple of Cuban gastronomy like Miami's Versailles restaurant offers non-Cuban specialties on its menu, including churrasco, a thick Argentine cut of steak. Strolling Mexican-style mariachi bands are common, but the musicians are often Colombians. More and more, there are households where the spouses hail from different Spanish-speaking countries or backgrounds.

Marco Rubio, a Cuban American, knows firsthand about the blending of Latin cultures. The 33-year-old Coral Gables attorney and Republican majority leader in the state House is married to a Colombian American who used to be a cheerleader for the Miami Dolphins. They have two children.

"I describe my two daughters, Amanda, 4, and Daniella, 2, as Colombanas—half Cuban, half Colombian, and 100% American," Rubio said. "I myself never ate an arepa (a Colombian specialty made of cornmeal) until I married Jeanette." On the other hand, Rubio said, "any Hispanic who lives any length of time in Miami ends up at a Cuban bakery and picks up some Cuban words.

"What you get is all those different Hispanic cultures melding into one 'Miami' culture," Rubio said. "America has always been about taking the best of other parts of the world, the best of other cultures."

The New Face of Appalachia

By Kim Cobb
Houston Chronicle, October 22, 2006

She sits toward the back of the storefront church, her silver hair and aquarium-blue eyes shining in the low light.

Elaine Solomon likes the way the place makes her feel. She likes the families swaying, clapping and singing with raised hands to a ranchera-style praise band.

"*Su santo espiritu ha llegado, oh dulce espiritu de Dios*," they sing. Your holy Spirit has arrived, oh sweet Spirit of God.

There are plenty of places to find God in Morristown but few places for a 70-year-old woman to learn Spanish. So there she is, week after week at a Latino Baptist church, learning the language of the newcomers, the people some of her neighbors call "the invasion."

"Somebody needs to learn to talk to these people," she said.

Latino immigration has been changing the face of the United States for decades. Immigrants follow certain jobs, and the fastest-growing Latino communities these days are in Southeastern states such as Tennessee.

But no one in Morristown expected it to come here. Framed by the Appalachian Mountains and an insular culture of mostly white residents, much of east Tennessee is an old, familiar photo in a worn frame: winding roads, clapboard houses and mile after mile of farm-furrowed green.

Even in thoroughly modern Morristown, tied to the rest of the world through manufacturing, the arrival of "these people" is quickly changing a region that has clung to a shared cultural and ethnic identity since the 1700s.

This kind of change can feel threatening, all mixed up in knotty questions about legal and illegal, assimilation, job loss and fear. At the very least, people are conflicted.

There's also been a lot of sign-waving and harsh words aimed in the past year at illegal immigrants here. Morristown's police chief is uneasy about the potential for violence, thanks to gut-stirring visits from the Tennessee Volunteer Minutemen and the Ku Klux Klan.

"Little Mexico"

Hamblen County's resident Latino population jumped from a few hundred to as many as 10,000 in the past decade, and the Pew Hispanic Center estimates that more than half the immigrants arriving in southeastern communities are illegal. Cumberland Avenue on the town's south side has been transformed into a commercial strip dominated by Latino restaurants, specialty stores and used-car lots.

"I mean, right here, where our church is, is Little Mexico," said the Rev. William Burton of Iglesia Bautista La Gran Comision, or The Great Commission Baptist Church.

The pastor is an exuberant, round-faced white man who speaks the Spanish he learned as a missionary in Venezuela with a decidedly Tennessee accent. His congregation began as a Bible study group at another Southern Baptist church. The study group grew, and Burton eventually began offering an early service on Sunday mornings in Spanish.

But, the young minister said, his devotion to the newcomers created resentment among some of the church's established members. It was never put into words, but Burton felt the challenge to choose "between us and them."

"Of course, my heart was with 'them,'" he said.

Burton quit and took his new flock with him. Six years down the road, La Gran Comision is flourishing in a salmon-colored stucco building that used to be a grocery store.

And Solomon, whose roots in Appalachia run deep, is soaking up Spanish.

A retired practical nurse, Solomon works part time at a pregnancy-support center with a growing list of Spanish-speaking Latina clients. She lowers her voice and adds quickly, "We're anti-abortion."

Solomon is among the half-dozen whites who attend Burton's church services.

Yes, Solomon agrees, Morristown is insular. But she also sees similarities between the Latinos and the region's historically Scots-Irish and German population that some might not see in themselves.

"I guess in a way they are like Appalachians," Solomon said. "I never considered myself Appalachian until I read a book called *40 Acres and No Mule*, and I discovered I am Appalachian. You have a feeling for the land and an attachment to the, you know, between families.

"We're clannish—and I see the same thing in these people."

Perception vs. Reality

There are plenty of people here who feel as if they're being run over at the intersection of demographic and economic change.

"I don't want my grandson to have to learn Spanish—he's an American," fumed Judy Mitchell, whose family has lived here for more than 200 years.

Morristown does not fit the Appalachian stereotype of quaint villages and hillbilly shacks.

It's a factory town with the usual Ameri-bland assortment of burger joints, drugstores, a Wal-Mart. For generations, the spectacular mountain greenery visible from the highest points in town was a wall between Morristown and change.

But change has come. Now, when residents say they don't like to travel the area along South Cumberland Avenue after dark, they mean they fear the newest arrivals who frequent the Latino businesses there.

That fear may be overblown. Roger Overholt, the chief of police, said the crime rate among Latinos is not much different from that of their neighbors. Cases of public intoxication and cars being abandoned after accidents increased with the arrival of Latinos, he said. But an education campaign about American law reduced the problem.

Morristown averages one homicide a year. There were five in 2002, which Overholt called "probably our worst year." None involved Latinos killing whites.

Still, the perception of danger is strong.

"I came out of South Florida . . . because I couldn't speak the [Spanish] language and I had to carry a gun," property manager Ronald Barwick said. "This was not Florida. People worked on a handshake and spoke English. [Now] the illegals have really taken over this county."

Settling In, Sort of

The immigrants rub shoulders with the whites in jobs and stores and schools. But life is what happens at home and in church.

You can't marry in Hamblen County without a Social Security number—an obvious hurdle for the many immigrants who don't have one. So on a Saturday afternoon in June, as he frequently does, the Rev. Burton journeyed to nearby Granger County, where there is no such restriction, to marry two young members of his congregation.

It was an outdoor ceremony held under a spreading magnolia tree—what Burton called "a real Southern wedding" except for the Mexican tradition of wrapping a lasso around the couple as a symbol of their union.

Some Latino residents said Morristown is becoming more comfortable. Even with the occasional protests mounted against illegal immigrants, they can shop, dine and worship in places where Spanish is spoken.

And there is work.

Juan Madrigal, his wife, Erica, and baby daughter Zuri are regulars at Burton's Thursday night services, basking in the sense of family they find in the congregation. Public protests against illegal immigrants do not concern them.

"We're not afraid because if they deport us, they'll deport us to our country," Madrigal said.

It's hard to think about whether they prefer life here to their old home. Madrigal was only 17 when he left Mexico.

"We're happy here," Madrigal said. "You get used to a community and a house and a way of life, and if we go back to Mexico we're going to miss this place."

But in the white community, it's hard for some people to separate uneasiness about the new population from resentment over the slow demise of the old way of life.

Global Give-and-Take

In recent years, Hamblen County learned what globalism meant by watching its biggest factories shut down and many good-paying jobs move to cheap-labor countries—such as Mexico.

But free trade in Morristown cuts both ways.

> But in the white community, it's hard for some people to separate uneasiness about the new population from resentment over the slow demise of the old way of life.

Many Mexican farming communities suffered financially when forced to compete with American agricultural products. The stream of immigrants to the United States from farm states such as Michoacan and Oaxaca grew in the mid-1990s as word spread about low-skill factory and agriculture jobs in east Tennessee.

So here's what it looks like from some corners of Morristown: The jobs went to Mexico, then Mexico came to Morristown.

Residents of Southwest border states have long been immersed in the debate over illegal crossings. Texas has had a large Latino population for more than a century, most of it legal and destined to become the majority by 2040.

Morristown, by contrast, is mired in culture shock.

"You know, I thought our community was doing well," Burton said. "And then our county commissioner, Tom Lowe, started all that nonsense about wanting to charge the federal government for so many illegals."

About 85 percent of the Hamblen County budget is spent on the local school district. Lowe started asking pointed questions about how much it costs to educate students who cannot speak English.

Lowe, a flush-faced pharmacist with curly, strawberry-blonde hair, has plenty of critics. But the town's "fence-sitters" began openly supporting his calls for enforcement of immigration law, Lowe said, after they saw Latinos waving Mexican flags at pro-immigrant rallies.

"I think America is in great distress over this," he said.

Effects of Extremism

Turmoil in Morristown started when a group calling itself the Tennessee Volunteer Minutemen began organizing against the illegal population. At least, that is the view of Lisa Barba, a regional organizer for the Tennessee Immigration and Refugee Rights Coalition.

Lowe is tired of hearing allegations from city leaders that the Klan is involved in the anti-illegal immigrant movement here. It's a smear, he thinks, to paint everyone concerned about illegal immigration as racist.

Burton thinks the white community is learning to bend with the changes, but he expects real acceptance of the newcomers may be slow in coming.

"We are a closed culture," the clergyman said. "I mean, our mountains have separated us culturally from the rest of the U.S. It's not necessarily just Latinos—it's anybody from, you know, the north or any place else that is not from here."

II. Hispanic Americans and the Immigration Debate

Editor's Introduction

Throughout the 230-year history of the American republic, the population has been continually augmented through immigration. Indeed, major migrations—whether from Ireland, Italy, Germany, Eastern Europe, or elsewhere—have reshaped American society, making it decidedly more vibrant, diverse, and prosperous as the years have passed. Yet these immigrants were hardly welcomed with open arms. Indeed, with each new influx of people from foreign shores, fear and resentment arose in certain sectors of the native-born population. Much of the concern was economic: Some worried that immigrants were driving down wages, doing more work for less, and taking jobs from natural-born citizens; others felt that immigrants were not learning English fast enough or contributed to higher crime rates. But certain fears were more existential in nature: Many nativists held that the racial, cultural, and religious make-up of the newcomers was incompatible with and thus a grave threat to the American way of life. The Roman Catholicism of Irish and Italian immigrants, not to mention their presumed racial inferiority and political radicalism, for example, excited profound anxiety within the country's predominantly Protestant population.

Though the major source of immigration has shifted away from Europe in recent decades, the fears generated among American citizens about these newcomers have remained eerily familiar. Still, there are those who worry about the structural differences they perceive between the predominantly Hispanic immigration of today and earlier influxes. First, there is the issue of legality: Until 1891, the United States had open borders—anyone who wished to come was legally free to do so. Gradually, however, laws were passed to restrict the number of potential citizens allowed into the country. These limitations, combined with the geographical proximity of Mexico to the United States and the precarious economic and political structures south of the border, have resulted in what many see as an immigration crisis. This predicament is replete with millions of undocumented workers (often referred to as "illegal" immigrants), security concerns, and a blossoming nativist backlash typified by the Minutemen, a group of citizens who have taken it upon themselves to police the borders.

The articles in this chapter provide an overview of the present situation, examining both the existential concerns about Hispanic immigration as well as the more mundane worries regarding language skills and economics. The first selection, "Assimilation, Past and Present," addresses the former apprehension, as Robert A. Levine considers the history of immigration in the United States and the fears that accompanied each succeeding influx. He ultimately concludes, "It is clear that Hispanic immigration is part and parcel of broader American patterns of assimilation and integration. Their story, like that of the Irish, Jews, and Italians before them, is an American story." While offering a somewhat different perspective in the next piece, "Back to the Future," David Frum worries that Hispanic immigrants are not effectively assimilating and that this could have "unsettling long-term political and economic consequences for the United States."

In "English Spoken Here?" Sydney J. Freedberg, Jr. explores the language issue as it relates to Hispanic Americans. Despite nativist fears of Spanish supplanting English as the country's "official" language, Freedberg shows that rates of English mastery are surprisingly high among second-generation Hispanics, and thus the language controversy is perhaps overblown.

The plight of undocumented workers has emerged as one of the more divisive topics in American discourse. Many argue that border controls should be tightened, undocumented workers deported, and those who hire them punished. On the other side, some call for an amnesty that would grant a path to citizenship for the undocumented. In "Illegal—but Essential," David Streitfeld examines the debate, noting the essential role undocumented workers play in the economy, as well as the degree to which they and their children—illegal or not—have become part of the American landscape.

Offering a more personal perspective, John Spong, in "My Life as an Illegal," describes his experience as an undocumented worker and the life he has managed to provide for his family. In the final piece in this chapter, "Divided over Immigration," Jennifer Delson explores the rifts that exist within the Latino community over undocumented workers. Though the Minuteman Project and other anti-immigrant groups are decidedly Caucasian in composition, a small but vocal minority of native-born Hispanics has waded into the debate to voice their support for stricter enforcement of immigration laws.

Assimilation, Past and Present

BY ROBERT A. LEVINE
PUBLIC INTEREST, SPRING 2005

Is America's Anglo-Protestant-African-Catholic-Indian-German-Irish-Jewish-Italian Slavic-Asian society in danger of "Hispanicization?" The obvious answer is "no." Every major new addition to American society has been viewed in its time as a potential agent of change. And this view has been correct: American society has continuously evolved. But "change" is not a synonym for "danger," and in no case has the essential fabric of America been endangered. Nor is it by the latest influx of mainly Mexican Hispanics.

Acculturation has always been a two-way street in the United States. The major waves of immigrants into this country, starting with the Irish in 1845, did not become Anglo-Protestants like those who colonized the eastern seaboard, declared independence, and wrote the Constitution and the Bill of Rights. (Of course, given the large numbers—and, yes, influence—of blacks, the colonies and states had never been fully Anglo-Protestant anyhow.) But the newcomers did become Americans, and in the process, Anglo-Protestant society changed too.

Although the answer to the question about endangerment is "no," it is not, however, "Of course not." Those who fear the current Hispanic influx contend that this time things will be different. True, the same has been stated about every previous wave of immigrants, wrongly as it happens. But perhaps the case of Hispanics really is different: After the boy's false cries of "wolf," the wolf did come and eat a number of villagers, including the boy. But in our case, the wolf is not crossing the Rio Grande and the Sonoran Desert. The Hispanic immigration is in fact different, but it is no more different than the other ones were from each other, and the republic is not in danger, at least not from this quarter.

I will focus on the effects of the current large-scale Mexican immigration on American society and life, because that is where the fears are. As put by Harvard political scientist Samuel P. Huntington in his recent book *Who Are We? The Challenges to America's National Identity*:

> Mexican immigration is leading toward the demographic *reconquista* of areas Americans took from Mexico by force in the 1830s and 1840s. . . . It is also blurring the border between Mexico and America, introducing a very different culture, while

also producing the emergence, in some areas, of a blended society and culture, half-American and half-Mexican.

These concerns are directed at the Mexican immigration (or sometimes at the broader Hispanic immigration), not at other related issues or problems: the parallel Asian immigration that is both smaller, more highly educated, and thus more easily assimilated; the environmental and other effects of overall population increases; or the legal and political issues surrounding undocumented immigrants. The issue raised by the critics is the composition of the American population, not its size or the effects on homeland security of a porous border. These are issues in their own right, and would have to be addressed separately.

Huntington provides an important analytical dichotomy, dividing the elements of "American identity" between "creed"—ideology, having to do mainly with our political institutions—and the underlying "culture" that structures the society in which we live. I'll start with a brief discussion of previous mass immigrations—Irish, Eastern European Jews, and Italians—as a background for the examination of the impact of the Mexican immigration first on America's creed—which remains safe—and then on our culture—which the newcomers will change, as newcomers always have.

The Irish, Jews, and Italians

Until 1845, the 13 colonies and then the United States were essentially the Anglo-Protestant societies of rosy recall. There were some others—English Catholics and Germans, in particular—but the generalization held. Starting with the Irish potato famine of 1845 and the consequent mass migration to the United States, however, things began to change rapidly. The remainder of the nineteenth century and the beginning of the twentieth saw three waves of immigration comparable in size to the current Hispanic influx. After the Irish, a new wave beginning in the 1880s and lasting until the threshold of the First World War brought in Italians (and a smaller number of Eastern European Catholics), and Eastern European Jews. The two million Irish who entered in the 1840s became about 10 percent of the American population; by 1925 Italian Americans and Jews together constituted a somewhat larger proportion of the population. It should be noted that the peak proportion of foreign-born Americans was 14.8 percent in 1890; in 2000, it was 11.2. We have a way to go before we match even our own immigrant past.

All three migrations were different from one another; all three were absorbed in similar ways—"Americanizing" the newcomers into a society that changed simultaneously by adapting to the immigrants. For each of the three groups, the process was a long one—from 50 or so years for substantial acceptance to about a century for full assimilation.

Starting in 1845, the signs went up, "No Irish Need Apply." The anti-Catholic Know-Nothing party burgeoned nationally, and Irishmen were caricatured as "monkeys." Virulent anti-Catholicism persisted through the last gasp of the Ku Klux Klan in the 1920s; it did not disappear (almost) until the 1960 election of John F. Kennedy to the presidency. Long before that, however, the Irish had essentially assimilated: Al Smith's 1928 presidential candidacy was defeated partially by the Klan, but the very fact that the Democrats nominated him indicates widespread acceptance.

However, the culture the Irish assimilated into over the course of a century was not the "pure" Anglo-Protestant society of 1845. The assimilation process itself made America partly Irish. Irish cops became the norm in many cities, and later, Fordham-educated FBI agents spread across the country. Catholicism, still largely Irish-led, has changed from "the Enemy" to merely another religious denomination, the largest one. St. Patrick's Day is practically an American festival. On many political issues today, Catholics are allied with evangelical Protestants against cultural "liberalism."

The parallel immigrations of Italians and other Catholics from Eastern Europe and of Eastern European Jews beginning in the 1880s followed a similar pattern. It would be 50 to 100 years for the Mediterranean laborers and the exotically dressed Talmudists to become the contractors, business CEOs, college presidents, novelists, and entertainers of the present. And this assimilation was strengthened by intermarriage: By 1990, the intermarriage rate for Italians had reached 60 percent; the corresponding figure for Jews is about 50 percent. But their assimilation changed America. The culture of Martin Scorsese and Philip Roth, former president Lee Iacocca of Chrysler and president Lawrence Summers of Harvard, the pizza and the bagel, is not the culture of Nathaniel Hawthorne and the barrel of salt pork, let alone the England of Samuel Johnson.

More importantly, these three immigrant waves have not degraded the American political creed or our essential political institutions. Political absorption can be measured by congressional statistics. The House of Representatives elected in 2002 had 26 Jews and 25 Italian Americans; nobody bothers to count the Irish any more, nor, given intermarriage, would that be possible. Senatorial statistics, however, are even more revealing. It is easy for individual congressional districts to become dominated by ethnic majorities and to elect their representatives accordingly. But none of the three immigrant groups has become a majority in any state and thus election to the Senate marks a more substantial degree of assimilation to the political creed. A few Irishmen were elected to the Senate before the Civil War, but it took 60 years, to the first decade of the twentieth century, for the cumulative number to reach five. That number mounted to 25 by the 1940s; after that it became too difficult to count, and nobody cared anyhow. The Jewish experience was parallel. It took until the 1970s, 90 years after the start of mass immigration, to elect the tenth Jewish senator; by the 1990s, the cumulative number had reached 26.

There have been fewer Italian-American senators, about 10 by the 1990s. Writers about immigration and assimilation frequently talk in terms of Jews and Italians as a single wave, but the intermediate paths of the two groups have been very different. The vast majority of Eastern European Jews came from large or small urban areas in the Russian "Pale of Settlement," including Poland and the Baltic areas, and from adjacent areas of eastern and central Europe. They seldom worked the land. And their biblical and Talmudic traditions brought them to Ellis Island as small business people, craftsmen such as tailors, and most importantly, scholars and debaters. These characteristics helped Jews take better advantage of America's educational opportunities than Italian immigrants.

Italians of the mass migration came as illiterate peasants from the southern *Mezzogiorno*, by far the poorest region of the newly unified

---

In 2002, there were 37.4 million Hispanics in the United States, approximately 13.0 percent of the total population.

Italy. They typically made their way as pick-and-shovel construction laborers in work gangs organized by *padroni*, an echo of the near-feudal system from which they came. They were close to their churches, in separate parishes disdained by the Irish who had by then established themselves. Education was not a priority. For these reasons, Italian assimilation was slower than Jewish assimilation, the Mafia outlasted the Jewish gangs, and the first really well-known Italian-American executive of a non-ethnic company, Lee Iacocca, came relatively late in the game. And fewer Italians were elected to the Senate, though it should be noted that the first Italian-American candidate for vice president of the United States, Geraldine Ferraro, preceded the first Jew, Joe Lieberman, by 16 years.

The Jewish experience is better known, and many of the doubts about the new Hispanic mass immigration may be based on an implicit and misleading comparison to the relatively rapid rise of Jews in America. But in fact, the Italian experience is the more relevant comparison for Mexican Americans, and thus should be kept in mind as we consider their place in America today.

Mexicans by the Numbers

We should begin by being clear about the basic data. In 2002, there were 37.4 million Hispanics in the United States, approximately 13.0 percent of the total population. Twenty-five million were of Mexican origin—two thirds of the Hispanics and about 8.5

percent of the total. The Census of 1970 was the first to separate out the Hispanic population, which was 4.5 percent of the total, with about 3.0 percent of Mexican origin. That could not have been much greater than the mid 1880s after the annexation of Texas and the conquests of the Mexican War. The mass migration began in the 1970s; by 1980, the percentages had nearly doubled, with the rate of increase slowing down to reach the current numbers.

Both the size and the rate of increase concern those worried about "Hispanicization." But neither is unprecedented. As has been noted, in relative terms the size of the foreign-born population of the United States is substantially smaller than at the height of the immigration at the turn of the twentieth century. And in the middle of the nineteenth century, the Irish population mounted even more rapidly.

Another statistic, while less certain, might be a cause for some disquiet: The Census Bureau projects the Hispanic portion of the population to rise to 24.4 percent by 2050. Applying the two-thirds ratio,

---

The Census Bureau projects the Hispanic portion of the population to rise to 24.4 percent by 2050.

---

that would put the population of Mexican origin at about 16 percent. Since Mexico is the largest and closest source of Hispanic emigrants to the United States, perhaps 20 percent would be a better round number. That figure is unprecedented for a single nation of origin to the United States, although in the 1920s, Jews and Italian Americans together did approach that level. Such an estimate is a sober quantification of the alarmists' fear of a foreign country, across a river and desert rather than an ocean, pumping new people into our comfortable America.

But 20 percent reached in 80 years beginning from the 1970 start of the Hispanic immigration represents neither a large number nor a rapid rate of increase. Although the long-run percentage is higher than for the previous waves, the time to get there approximates or exceeds the time it took for each of the earlier groups to reach an effectively full assimilation. The real issue is whether the Mexicans will take a similar route of assimilating into a society that is simultaneously accommodating them.

Playing Politics?

If the influx of Mexicans—or of Latinos, or any other group—were to threaten the basic liberal democratic institutions by which the United States has governed itself since 1789, such a threat would indeed call into question the entire range of policies affecting immigration, assimilation, and citizenship. Fortunately, no such threat exists. Mexican Americans are being absorbed into the political process at similar rates and with similar effects as earlier immigrant groups, and America's political creed and institutions remain as they have been.

Looking first at the congressional statistics, the current House of Representatives has 25 Hispanics, about two thirds of whom are of Mexican background. This means that Mexican-American political assimilation is moving along at a faster rate than that of Jews or Italians in similar periods of time. Entry into the Senate has of course been slower. Aside from New Mexico, a state with a unique and deep Mexican background, which has elected Mexican-American senators, no Latinos joined the Senate until 2004. In that year, however, Cuban-American Republican Mel Martinez was elected from Florida, a state in which Cuban Americans are far from a majority; he was joined by Mexican-American Democrat Ken Salazar from Colorado, which remains heavily Anglo.

The number of Mexican and other Latino holders of lesser offices suggests that others will follow into the Senate and perhaps national elective offices. Governor Bill Richardson of New Mexico, whose mother was Mexican American, had been mentioned as a Democratic vice presidential or presidential candidate. California has a Mexican-American lieutenant governor and is on its second Mexican-American speaker of the state assembly. Almost a quarter of the state's legislators—29 of 120—are of Mexican background. In 2001, a Hispanic candidate almost won the mayoralty of Los Angeles; four years later, he and another are challenging the incumbent. As these examples demonstrate, Hispanic involvement in American politics is thus following a perfectly normal pattern for ethnic groups, albeit perhaps a little faster.

If the new Hispanics in power carried with them a radical or separatist political agenda, such rapid penetration could be dangerous. But this is emphatically not the case. Hispanic radicals do exist—occasionally, though less than in the past, one hears of calls for "Aztlan," a separate Mexican America. The mainstream of Hispanic politics is well within the American consensus, somewhat to the right for Florida's Cuban Americans, somewhat to the left for the Mexican Americans of California and Texas. As our newly appointed attorney general Alberto Gonzales shows, however, none of these groups is monolithic. Gonzalez is a politically conservative Mexican American from Texas. Indeed, the political diversity of Hispanics is borne out by the movement of a significant portion of Hispanic voters toward George W. Bush and the Republican Party in the recent election.

Hispanic politicians do, of course, represent Hispanic views and interests. Mexican Americans are disproportionately poor, so their representatives tend to favor liberal social programs. Other issues are more specifically Hispanic: benefits going to illegal aliens and bilingual education, for example. But Hispanics are not univocal either on specifically "Hispanic causes" or on most other issues. A significant number have been converting from the Catholicism of their birth to evangelical Protestantism. Many of these join in the emphasis given by evangelicals to "moral issues," as compared to the economic issues that typically motivate people with lower incomes.

Upward Mobility?

If Mexicans were simply coming to the United States to take advantage of welfare while failing to improve on their meager educations, that too could be a major cause for worry. This is not the case, however, nor do most opponents of immigration claim that it is. While some Mexican immigrants do end up on welfare and many who enter at mature ages do find difficulty in raising their educational levels, the overwhelming motivation for entering the United States is employment. And they and their descendants do understand that education is necessary for all but the lowest-skilled jobs.

Although most of the data show improvement in employment, skills, and education, controversy concerns the rates of improvement. Some believe that progress is too slow or slowing down. Comparisons are made to other immigrant groups: One analyst, for example, complains that "Non-Mexican (working) immigrants have an average wage income of $21,000 a year. Mexican immigrants have an average wage income of $12,000 a year. The typical Mexican immigrant has less than an eighth-grade education."

Such comparisons to parallel groups of immigrants are close to meaningless, however. Mexican immigrants are from lower socioeconomic strata than the educated Asians whose children do so well, or the middle-class Cubans who have fled Castro. Thirty-five years after the beginning of the mass immigrations at the end of the nineteenth century, the same unfavorable comparisons could have been made between Jews and Italians. Without a doubt, Mexicans are more disadvantaged than other contemporary entrants. The real comparison, however, should not be to Asians but to the earlier Italians. The very fact of continued Mexican improvement implies strongly that the employment and educational courses of the two groups are parallel.

History suggests, therefore, that the seeming slowness of Mexican improvement on these indices should not be of major concern. And in any case, it is far from established that such improvement is slow; the controversy provides a nice example of difficulties in interpreting statistics. Huntington, for instance, cites an analysis by RAND Corporation economist James P. Smith. According to Huntington:

> Smith's careful analysis . . . presents figures for the adjusted wage values of Mexican-American men as percentages of native white men's lifetime earnings. Those for the third-generation descendants of Mexicans born in the 1860s were 74.5 percent. The adjusted wage values of third-generation Mexican-Americans whose immigrant parents were born between 1910

and 1920 had risen to only about 80 percent. . . . As with educational levels, the second generation does markedly better than the first, but then progress falters.

But Smith's own view, in the same document cited by Huntington, challenges such an interpretation:

The conventional view regarding Hispanic immigrants' inability to secure a better life for their children and grandchildren has been pessimistic. . . . These fears are unwarranted: 2nd and 3rd-generation Hispanic men have made great strides in closing the economic gaps with native whites. The reason is simple— each successive generation has been able to close the schooling gap with native whites which then has been translated into generational progress in incomes.

Smith's data bear out his contention of generational convergence. For example, Mexican immigrant men now in their late forties are 5.59 years of education short of native American white men; the sons of these immigrants are only 1.04 years short. Mexicans now in their early eighties (the most recent for whom two-subsequent-generation data are available) were 4.05 years short, their sons 1.77 years short, and their grandsons half that at .82 years. Wages followed a similar pattern albeit more slowly: the 40-year-olds earned about two-thirds as much as whites, their sons seven-eighths; the 80-year-olds and their sons improved similarly, but their grandsons gained little over their own fathers. Education is the future. Smith's data show that Mexican Americans are generally moving forward.

Ketchup vs. Salsa

If political and socioeconomic factors look basically promising, the cultural question is more complicated and harder to measure—as it always is. The influx of Mexicans and other Hispanics will in fact change America's culture. The twenty-first century will differ from the twentieth as the twentieth differed from the nineteenth, and the second half of the nineteenth differed from the first half, when American culture could have been accurately described as "Anglo-Protestant." Some have mourned each change; some still do.

Mexican Americans have not yet begun to penetrate American "high culture," nor should that be expected for a while. The Roths and Scorseses, the Yehudi Menuhins and Ezio Pinzas made major contributions at that level only three quarters of a century or so after the beginning of the Jewish and Italian waves. But in more popular culture, Mexicans and other Latinos have already made a deep impression. Food is not a bad initial index. Chains of Mexican food stands and more formal restaurants dot the road and claim their places in shopping malls; the chili-burger is on the menu of most hamburger joints; the taco has become as American as the bagel and the pizza. Sales of salsa outstrip those of ketchup. Similarly, Mexican popular music (also called salsa) and other Latino streams have not only joined into popular music but have changed it.

In religion, Mexicans and other Hispanics are not only changing the face of the Catholic church, but the growing number of Hispanic evangelicals is expanding on the Anglo-Protestant base of that

> Hispanic political power is converging toward the national mean, not splitting away from it.

movement (the American roots of which are of course in part black.) This is an illustration of how immigrants frequently end up not only transforming the culture but reinvigorating older American institutions.

Two Nations?

Most of the evidence suggests that the mass Mexican immigration is, and is likely to remain, within standard American historical patterns. One unprecedented characteristic of the Mexican ingress is that the nation sending the emigrants is right across the border, easy to cross relative to the oceans traversed by the previous immigrations. The earlier waves reached high tide and then receded; the Mexicans can keep coming. And the numbers they may reach, charge some critics, will bring about a separate cultural-linguistic unit within the United States.

That would indeed be new and dangerous, but is also unlikely to happen. One more demographic projection qualifies the feared 20 to 25 percent of the United States population, and sets the context for the absorption of the new Hispanics. According to researchers Robert Suro and Jeffrey Passel:

> As it continues to grow, the composition of the Hispanic population is undergoing a fundamental change. Births in the United States are outpacing immigration as the key source of growth. Over the next twenty years, this will produce an important shift in the makeup of the Hispanic population.

Since 60 percent of the Hispanic population is already native-born, most of the new Hispanics are old Hispanics—American citizens by right of birth—and that proportion will increase at an accelerated pace. That in itself could be cause for alarm rather than comfort; it puts *them* in a position to seize power in all or part of the country. But, as discussed above, Hispanic political power is converging toward the national mean, not splitting away from it. And the evidence about the American generations of Hispanics is that they too are converging. This is demonstrated along three dimensions, language, intermarriage, and geographical diffusion.

English is the language of the United States. Small (e.g., German) exceptions have been allowed; as new immigrants, including but not limited to Hispanics, have been entering in large numbers, transitory exceptions have become relatively frequent more recently (and very unpopular). But if long-run Hispanic enclaves—the equivalent of Quebec's *Parlez français, tous qui entrent!*—were to establish themselves, the critics would have a real point. The bilingual society does not work well in Canada, and would work much worse in the United States. Switzerland is an exception, not the rule.

The United States is in little danger of becoming such a bilingual society, however. Political arguments over a bilingual America frequently center on the issue of bilingual education: Should students not proficient in English be taught in their first language—usually Spanish—as well as English, so that they can keep up in school? Or should they be taught only in English because they will never learn it well enough to live in an English-speaking society if they can fall back on their mother tongues if they want?

The question is a good one; the evidence on whether bilingual or English-only instruction works better is mixed and still coming in. Unfortunately, extremes on both sides have distorted the issue. Many advocates of English-only believe that the real motive of those pushing bilingual education is the preservation of Spanish as an alternative language, and it is true that some bilingual advocates want just that. In the total electorate, the English-only group is much larger, so California and other states have passed referendums dictating English as the sole acceptable language of instruction. The new laws have enough safety valves, however (e.g., parents can request exceptions), that they are not very well enforced, and both types of instruction are frequently used. And because the goal of learning English is so important for Hispanic students and parents, and because the overall evidence is ambiguous, such a mixture seems pragmatically to be the best solution.

In any case, the bilingual education debate is really a symbolic issue. The real question for the America-as-two-nations doomsayers is whether Spanish is becoming an alternate language for large groups of people. The strong evidence is that it is not. Mexicans and other Hispanic immigrants find English difficult to learn, and stick to Spanish in their families and among themselves, using English with some difficulty when they have to. But the next generations are fluent in both, tending in fact toward English only. Some Hispanic politicians have had to learn Spanish because they never picked up enough to campaign comfortably in Hispanic enclaves.

Observations like these are supplemented and backed up by more quantifiable data: In the first (immigrant) generation of Latinos, 72 percent speak primarily Spanish, 24 percent are bilingual, and only 4 percent are English dominant. In the second generation, only 7 percent stick to their Spanish, with the remaining 93 percent equally divided between bilingual and English-speaking. The third generation shows statistically zero Spanish-only speakers, with 78 percent being English-only. Among Mexicans and those of Mexican descent living in the United States who have been here less than 10 years, 30 percent are bilingual, 68 percent Spanish-only. For Mexicans in the United States 21 years or more, the numbers had equalized—49 percent bilingual, 46 percent Spanish-only. But among those of Mexican descent who were born in the United States, almost none were Spanish-only; 54 percent were bilingual, 44 percent English only.

To sum up: The evidence shows that Mexicans and other Hispanics, after they come to the United States, move toward the use of English. Among their children born in the United States (who, as noted above, are becoming the predominant group), that direction becomes very powerful. There is no reason this should be surprising. They came for jobs. At the start, the jobs were in the fields and Spanish worked perfectly well; increasingly, the jobs are in manufacturing and the service sector in the cities, where Spanish-only doesn't work well at all. Economic incentives work very well in this

---

The evidence shows that Mexicans and other
Hispanics, after they come to the United States,
move toward the use of English.

---

case. Those who worry about America becoming linguistically divided into two nations extrapolate far too much from small controversies about *how* Hispanic kids can best learn English, arriving at unwarranted fears about *whether*.

Like the data on language, figures on intermarriage show steady acculturation. About 15 percent of Hispanic-origin husbands have wives of non-Hispanic origin. Since intermarriages are likely to be concentrated among the native-born 60 percent of the Hispanic population, the rate for native Hispanic Americans is likely to be higher, perhaps 25 percent. As noted, 90 years after the beginning of their mass migrations, the intermarriage rate for Jews and Italians was 50 to 60 percent. Hispanics seem to be headed in the same direction. For them, however, as with Irish and Italian Americans, intermarriage will lose definition: What does it mean when an intermarried family intermarries?

Finally, patterns of diffusion demonstrate that the Hispanic population is assimilating rapidly. As border states, California, Arizona, New Mexico, and Texas will remain the entry points for Mexicans. For that reason and because of the already large Hispanic populations and the relatively high birth rates among these populations, Hispanic concentrations are likely to increase.

But the data also show that Hispanics are not sticking together in the old Mexican territories, but are spreading into other more purely Anglo states, particularly the South. In the five years leading up to the Census of 2000, although Hispanics from abroad flowed into all states and regions, with California and Texas leading the rest, *internal* migration of Hispanics showed a very different pattern. Regionally, the Northeast lost a net 151,000 to other sections, the West lost 161,000; 56,000 of them moved to the Midwest, and an astounding 256,000 moved to the South. Within the South, Texas struck a balance between in- and out-migrants; North Carolina was the biggest gainer with 41,000.

Clearly, Hispanics in the United States are not sticking to themselves in tight Spanish-speaking enclaves, looking inward, walling themselves off against Anglos. Far from it. The dominant language is becoming English at a rapid rate; they are marrying non-Hispanics at a historically predictable rate, and they are diffusing into new regions of the country.

Continuity

The wave of Hispanic immigration that has been taking place for several decades—and that is certain to continue for many more—has changed the United States and will continue to do so. It has changed American culture, as have all the other immigrant waves. Each change has discarded some characteristics valued by some with older roots in America, but immigrants have revitalized other parts of our common culture.

Where those who welcome and those who fear change join together, however, is in the importance they give to the American creed—our Constitution and our democratic institutions. The evidence is that these are in no danger, at least not from Hispanic Americans. Taking a larger view, it is clear that Hispanic immigration is part and parcel of broader American patterns of assimilation and integration. Their story, like that of the Irish, Jews, and Italians before them, is an American story.

Back to the Future

By David Frum
National Review, July 3, 2006

Mexican immigrants like it in America. They are much more likely than other immigrants to rate life in the United States as superior to life in the country where they were born, according to survey research by Public Agenda in 2003. They come to work: They are much less likely than other immigrants to cite political freedom as the reason for their migration. They show near zero interest in radical politics: Aside from a few loony college professors, the mystic cause of reuniting the southwestern United States to Mexico seems to excite almost nobody. They crossed the desert to escape Mexico, not to rejoin it. Whatever is going on, it isn't a Reconquista.

So . . . good news, right? Assimilation is working? Not exactly. Mexican immigrants may like America, but they are having serious trouble joining it. Well into the second and third generations after arrival, they remain much poorer than other Americans—with unsettling long-term political and economic consequences for the United States.

Only 7 percent of Mexican immigrants arrive in the United States able to speak English. Few possess much formal education. These deficiencies shunt them into low-wage sectors of the economy. The economist George Borjas calculates that Mexican Americans earn almost 40 percent less than American-born workers with American-born parents. Low wages hold Mexican Americans in poverty—and the evidence suggests that their families will remain poor into the second and third generations.

Lacking English and formal education themselves, Mexican-American immigrants do not seem to attach much importance to their children's acquiring either. While 82 percent of immigrants from Europe feel that all immigrants should be expected to learn English, and even 61 percent of non-Mexican Latinos agree, only a bare majority of Mexican immigrants, 54 percent, think English essential, again according to the Public Agenda survey. While 67 percent of non-Mexican immigrants think that public-school classes should be taught exclusively in English, only 51 percent of Mexicans think so.

Perhaps unsurprisingly, the children of these migrants do not flourish in school. A Manhattan Institute study of the high-school class of 1998 found that only 54 percent of Hispanic students graduated with their class, as compared with nearly 80 percent of their white counterparts. These dropouts may later return to school or earn a high-school equivalency certificate. But they will have difficulty catching up to their classmates who finished on time. And of course the children of high-school dropouts are more likely to drop out in their turn.

Borjas points out that the differences in earnings between U.S. immigrant groups and the native population persist from generation to generation. Experience would suggest that if Mexican immigrants earn 40 percent less than natives, their children will earn 20 percent less, their grandchildren 10 percent less, and so on. That's not a reassuring estimate, but the reality may well be even worse.

> The Center for Immigration Studies has found . . . that today's immigrants do considerably worse than previous immigrants.

The "experience" Borjas cites is that of immigrant families settling in the United States in the 1930s, '40s, and '50s: the golden age of blue-collar America. Even if they did not speak much English, even if they did not possess much formal education, they could find work in a factory or on a dock that paid better relative to other sectors of the economy, and offered higher inflation-adjusted wages, than the same jobs today. Post-1970 America has become a much tougher environment for those without higher education. In 1970, a 30-year-old man with a college degree earned a little more than twice as much as his counterpart with a high-school diploma. By 1990, he earned three times as much. Today, the disparity gapes wider still.

The Center for Immigration Studies has found considerable evidence that today's immigrants do considerably worse than previous immigrants, decades after arrival. In 1970, only 25.7 percent of immigrants who had lived in the U.S. for ten to twenty years were poor, compared with 35.1 percent of natives. By 2000, 41.4 percent of long-settled immigrants were poor, as compared with 28.8 percent of natives.

Behind all these numbers is an emerging social reality. The immigration policies of the past two decades have imported into the United States a large population that will remain ill educated, incompletely fluent in English, and significantly poorer than the rest of the country well into the 2030s and 2040s. And President Bush's proposal to settle this population permanently—and to increase the flow of new migrants—will make the problems bigger, deeper, and more intractable.

It's troubling to turn on the television and see thousands of illegal immigrants marching behind the Mexican flag, chanting slogans that denounce America's right to control its borders. But I'd worry a lot less about the Republic of Aztlan than about a future in which the American economy rests on a linguistically distinct subclass of ill-educated low-wage workers.

Imagine America in 2031. That's the not-so-distant future: It's a date as far ahead of us as Ronald Reagan's first inauguration is behind us. Suppose the Bush immigration plan of 2006 or something like it has been enacted. Illegal aliens have been legalized; family-reunification and guest-worker programs continue to bring millions of Mexicans and Central Americans north.

In 2031, daily life for you and your children (if I may make a demographic assumption about you, reader) probably proceeds more or less as it does today. The roads are more crowded, real estate and gasoline probably more expensive, taxes higher, and government services worse. On the other hand, many onetime luxuries have steadily declined in price. Domestic-cleaning services like Merry Maids have proliferated, as have in-home childcare and eldercare, gardening services, prepared-meal services, and car detailing. Like Alicia Silverstone in Clueless, you have little need to know how to parallel park—everywhere you want to go, they have valet. In short: The southern California lifestyle has spread throughout the country.

But what of the migrants whose labor sustains your pleasantly seigniorial life?

How do they feel about their relative poverty—a poverty cushioned but not significantly ameliorated by the food stamps, Earned Income Tax Credits, housing subsidies, and Medicaid benefits for which they are now eligible? At first, perhaps, they didn't complain much. Life in the United States represented a huge improvement over life in Mexico or Central America. First-generation migrants worked too hard, felt too insecure, and trusted government too little to agitate for a better deal. But what of their American-born but ill-educated and low-wage children?

They have the vote. They have expectations of a better life. Will they not find politicians ready to mobilize them for a new era of populist redistributionism—a redistributionism made more powerful and more exciting by the ethnic and linguistic differences between haves and have-nots?

Certainly that is the future left-wing Democrats expect. Immigration reformers often express wonder that the political Left has welcomed an immigration whose main effect is to lower the wages of less-skilled workers, especially black men. But maybe the Left is playing a longer game here—where the short-term depression of living standards for working people becomes a necessary price to pay to reignite the radical economic movements that inflamed the United States from 1870 to 1940.

Americans have become so used to political and economic stability that they have forgotten that their country was once disgraced by the most violent and bloody labor conflicts on earth. These conflicts were often intensified by the ethnic differences between strikers and the American population at large—differences that exerted a follow-on effect in electoral politics. As Michael Barone observes in Our Country, his magisterial history of 20th-century American poli-

tics, outside the South the division between support for and opposi-
tion to Franklin Delano Roosevelt's New Deal was grounded on
ethnicity as much as social class, with old-stock Americans against
and immigrants and the children of immigrants in favor.

Politicians like Los Angeles mayor Antonio Villaraigosa plainly
hope that the trick can be repeated in this new century. As Harold
Meyerson wrote in The American Prospect, the "Latinoization [of
California] has also transformed California's fiscal politics." The
state that led the tax-rebellion movement in the late 1970s and fed
the national conservative political resurgence passed "a massive
$9.2 billion school bond measure and a $2 billion initiative for parks
and open-space preservation" in 1998, and reduced the power of
anti-tax voters to veto local-government bond measures. "With the
uptick in Latino voting . . . the gap between the voting public and
the people who need public services began to narrow."

Many conservative immigration advocates insist that Villaraigosa
and Meyerson have it wrong—that the migrants and their children
and grandchildren will be socially conservative and politically quies-
cent. It's worth noting, though, that Republican political professionals are ceasing to believe this: That's why so many of them, from
Karl Rove on down, now emphasize guest-worker programs as a
way to benefit from immigrant labor without having to face the consequences of immigrant votes.

But as the French and Germans have discovered, there is nothing
less temporary than a temporary worker. The migrants will settle,
will take up their political rights—and will use those rights to
advance their interests: interests that may sharply differ from those
of more-established inhabitants.

For more than half a century, American society has been divided
along lines of race. The most polarizing issues—busing, affirmative
action, welfare, crime—have explicitly or implicitly involved race.
Race has exerted so strong an influence that when new grievances
came along—the rights of women, of the disabled, of gays—the
grievance-bearers unselfconsciously squeezed and shoved their
demands into the forms left behind by the civil-rights battles of 30,
40, and 50 years before.

Race and race analogies so mesmerize us that we unthinkingly
assume that the challenges presented by immigration must fit into
this ancient envelope. It's almost impossible for us to imagine anything else—least of all something so antiquated, so remote as conflicts along the lines of class.

But everything old becomes new again. And it may well be that
the greatest threat from today's immigration is not that the United
States will be racially balkanized, but that it will relive a past in
which classes invoked ethnic solidarity in a struggle over wealth
and power. The danger is not that immigrants won't "Americanize."
They will. The danger is that they will reintroduce America to an
authentically American history that once seemed long and well forgotten.

English Spoken Here?

By Sydney J. Freedberg, Jr.
NATIONAL JOURNAL, January 7, 2006

If we can't even communicate, how can I trust you? Security concerns have bedeviled the Bush administration's ambitions for immigration reform ever since the September 11 attacks overshadowed President Bush's summit with Mexican President Vicente Fox that fateful week. Now, in the new year, House legislation calling for far stricter border security is headed for the floor of a reluctant Senate. Yet amid the contention, there is a surprising consensus on one fundamental goal: Every immigrant to this country should learn English.

"We're creating a nation of enclaves that can't communicate with each other—the single most unifying characteristic any civilization has is a common language," said Rep. Steve King, a conservative Republican from Iowa, where his German-born grandmother commanded her children to speak only English—and to teach her to speak it, too. King helped make English the official language of government business in Iowa and has introduced an "Official English" bill for the whole country.

"Learning English is an essential part of successfully integrating," echoed Clarissa Martinez, who came to the United States from Mexico at 15, speaking only Spanish, and is now head of state and local policy for the National Council of La Raza, a leading, and left-leaning, Hispanic activist group. "The question is how."

Even immigrants themselves will agree, though you may have to ask them in Spanish. In a recent series of focus groups with Spanish-speakers across the country, "the No. 1 goal that all of them referred to was a desire to learn English better, because it was the key to greater job opportunity," said professor Luis Ricardo Fraga, a Stanford University sociologist who was born and raised in Texas. "And they all said one of the major barriers is, we don't have enough opportunities to learn English."

That gap between aspiration and achievement is wide. The National Survey of Latinos, in 2002, found that 96 percent of Hispanics born here spoke English well—but the figure was only 28 percent among immigrants born abroad, and less than 16 percent among immigrants who arrived as adults age 18 or older. Children learn languages easily; adults do not. So the race is not just between immigration and assimilation: It is between immigrants and their own children, winner take America.

This country has run this race before, and integration has outpaced disintegration every time. Less of the population is foreign-born today (about 10 percent) than at the height of European immigration in 1910 (15 percent). Benjamin Franklin printed a German-language newspaper in 1732, and even into the 20th century, German-speakers in the Midwest, like King's grandmother, clustered in their own communities with their own churches, newspapers, even bilingual German-English schools. Those enclaves have long since dissolved. But will today's barrios?

People "wander into East Los Angeles and conclude that people aren't learning English and that we have problems; that's what's laughable," said professor Peter Skerry of Boston College and the Brookings Institution, and author of Mexican Americans: The Ambivalent Minority. The Germans, Poles, Italians, and others did not arrive reciting Shakespeare; why expect it of Mexicans? "It

---

"It takes time for immigrants to learn English, and lots of members of the first generation never quite get around to it."—Peter Skerry, Boston College and the Brookings Institution

---

takes time for immigrants to learn English, and lots of members of the first generation never quite get around to it," Skerry said. "The test is, what are their kids going to speak?"

But if that first generation pours in too fast, especially as illegal immigrants who face legal and linguistic barriers that bar them from the mainstream, it may form unassimilated enclaves that the second generation cannot escape. "When we get to about 20 [million] to 30 million illegal aliens, you will see de facto apartheid in the American Southwest," warned Victor Davis Hanson, a senior fellow with Stanford's Hoover Institution. "The number of arrivals from Mexico each year vastly outpaces the number who are assimilated as Americans. And facile comparisons with the Irish, Jews, Germans, etc., [are] intellectually dishonest."

A few key factors make Hispanics exceptional among immigrants in U.S. history—and Mexicans exceptional among Hispanics. Europeans and Asians may not speak English, but they have no alternative common language of their own—they come from many countries and dialects. In contrast, 20 of the 35 countries in this hemisphere are predominantly Spanish-speaking. Of the 38 million people in the United States who speak a language other than English at home, the 2000 census found that 28 million, or 73 percent, speak Spanish. Europeans and Asians may long for their homelands, but they have to cross oceans to go back; Latin Americans can drive. Mexican-Americans, especially, can make the trip many times a year, said Stanford professor Alberto Camarillo (born in Compton, Calif.): Just "go to the border on the Christmas holidays and see these massive caravans going back." And in contrast to, say, Chinese or Chileans, Mexican immigrants are disproportionately poor and poorly educated.

So, what is the critical mass of Mexicans that breaks the usual chain of assimilation and creates multigenerational enclaves cut off from English and from opportunity? A study released last September by the Urban Institute found that 70 percent of "Limited English Proficient" students are clustered in just 10 percent of public elementary schools; the majority of them were even U.S.–born, but to non-English-speaking parents. Other studies suggest, however, that "LEP" is hardly a life sentence.

According to an analysis of 2000 census data by University of New York (Albany) professor Richard Alba, 92 percent of second-generation Hispanic children speak English "well or very well," barely behind the 96 percent of second-generation Asians. Even among

---

According to an analysis of 2000 census data . . . 92 percent of second-generation Hispanic children speak English "well or very well."

---

children born in Mexico and now living in the United States, Alba found, 79 percent spoke English proficiently.

Individual immigrants become markedly more Americanized as they grow older, according to the University of California–led "Children of Immigrants Longitudinal Study," which repeatedly interviewed the same subjects over a decade. Researchers asked Mexican-born children attending public schools in San Diego if they preferred to speak English instead of Spanish. In 1992, when most of the children were 14 years old, 32 percent of them said they preferred to speak English; just three years later, 61 percent of the children preferred English. Hispanic immigrants seem to be learning English as eagerly as any others in U.S. history.

Don't relax just yet, though. Speaking English does not automatically make you feel "American."

"Even though language and identity are connected, identity issues are much more complicated," said professor Ruben Rumbaut, the Cuban-born University of California (Irvine) sociologist who directs the Children of Immigrants study. From 2001 to 2003, when researchers again interviewed these children of Mexican descent from San Diego (who were now in their early 20s and spread out across the country), less than 2 percent identified themselves as simply "American." Thirty percent simply called themselves "Mexican." And "Mexican-American" was the compromise choice of 37 percent, the largest single block; 29 percent said they were "Hispanic." In short, if forced to choose, almost two-thirds defined who they were without using the word "American" at all.

But they learned to do that from Americans. "When I interview recently arrived immigrants from Mexico, I ask what they think the terms 'Latino' or 'Hispanic' mean," Rumbaut explained. "They don't know. Those two words are made in the USA and imposed from the outside, just like 'Indians' and 'Negroes.' But the category 'Hispanic' is especially egregious—it de-Americanizes: Other groups get to be called 'Asian-American' or 'African-American' or 'American Indian,' [but not] 'Latin American.'"

"Over time, Mexicans do integrate into American society, but that isn't the end of the story," Boston College's Skerry said. "Some of them will want Spanish-language ballots or claim affirmative action—which doesn't mean they're un-American. Quite the contrary. Some of the most divisive things are often the most American things."

Would legislating an official national language make America less divided? When pressed, official-English advocates do not claim that banning Spanish will somehow help anyone learn English—and in fact, King's bill is so tightly restricted to government business, and so full of exceptions for "public health and safety; . . . any census; . . . victims of crimes or criminal defendants," and so on, that it would in practice ban very little.

Official English is not really aimed at immigrants at all: It is aimed over their heads as a salvo in a long-standing culture war over issues that go far beyond immigration, a war waged among American citizens and in English. "We've worshipped at the altar of multiculturalism," said King, who has also campaigned for "biblical values" in public education. "The cultural relativism being taught in our schools causes us to apologize for becoming Americans." Official English may not help immigrants assimilate, but it will certainly make a statement about which version of America they are supposed to assimilate to.

The problem is that symbolic legislation can backfire. The Children of Immigrants data show that from 1992 to 1995 (when most of the children were 17), the percentage who identified themselves as plain "American" fell by half, the percentage of "Mexican-Americans" and other hyphenated-American identities fell by a third, while the use of "Hispanic" increased and "Mexican" rocketed. Yet by 2001–03, the original proportions had mostly returned. What happened in between, Rumbaut argues, was Proposition 187, a controversial 1994 ballot initiative in California to cut off costly public services for illegal immigrants and their children. Young people who had never spent a lot of energy asserting a "Hispanic" or "Mexican" identity suddenly felt that "America" was rejecting them, and they would reject it in return.

When it comes to language and immigration, the symbolic battles tend toward bitter stalemate. But on the practical measures, there is a surprising consensus. At the conservative Hoover Institution, Hanson calls for "a radical English immersion and assimilation program" with "English immersion clinics." At the liberal La Raza, Martinez argues for "a proactive immigrant-integration approach [across] the education system." Chilean-born Mauro Mujica, the director of U.S. English Inc., the official-English lobby group, speaks admiringly of Israel's system of mandatory Hebrew classes for all new immigrants. "The government is far better off paying people for five or six months to learn the language," he said in strongly accented but fluent English. "Eventually, those people will repay it in taxes."

The debate over symbols may seize the nation. But the hard work of pulling America together faster than it can pull itself apart will be done in elementary classrooms and night schools around the country, one student at a time.

Illegal—but Essential

By David Streitfeld
Los Angeles Times, October 1, 2006

Shortly after dawn, the day laborers began gathering beneath a San Diego Freeway overpass in West Los Angeles.

A house painter pulled up in a pickup, looking for an assistant. He offered $12 an hour. A worker jumped in.

Next to arrive was a white-haired woman driving a Honda. Her garden needed a makeover. She'd pay $11 an hour. She departed with a second worker.

On the freeway above, commuters were heading to offices in Century City and El Segundo. Down here, at the West L.A. Community Job Center, arrangements were being made to remodel their living rooms, landscape their yards, rebuild their decks.

The work is undertaken by men from Mexico and Central America. Most are in this country illegally. The jobs, which last only a day or two and pay cash, are all but invisible to the state and federal governments. No one has to fill out paperwork, follow safety regulations or pay taxes.

Yet what happens here is far from marginal. The jobs that flow out of this day-laborer hiring spot—and from thousands of others around the state, some as informal as a street corner—are a pillar of California's economic strength.

To see why, check out Adrian Lopez, 20, who is kicking around a soccer ball as he waits. Lopez, who came here from the Mexican state of Oaxaca, is carrying in his Everest backpack a Sony Walkman from the Best Buy across the street.

It's got a CD by the Argentine group Los Enanitos Verdes inside, bought at a Ritmo Latino store. He has a bottle of Kirkland Premium Drinking Water, purchased at Costco, and a spare Old Navy shirt. He likes the grilled steak at Baja Bud's. He wasn't impressed by "Monster House."

"Immigrants buy everything here," Lopez said in Spanish.

The presence in the United States of Lopez and 12 million other illegal immigrants is one of the most contentious issues of the era. Hundreds of thousands of immigrants have repeatedly demonstrated this year for legal recognition, sparking a backlash from many native-born Americans. Congress has been stalemated between legalization advocates and those pushing punitive measures.

Economists are less divided. In the main, they say the American engines of industry and commerce have always been fueled by a steady supply of new arrivals. Immigrants, they contend, contribute to consumer spending and, instead of replacing native workers, create jobs.

"Overall, immigration has been a net gain for American citizens, though a modest one in proportion to the size of our $13-trillion economy," 500 economists wrote in an open letter to Congress on June 19.

Measuring the contributions of illegal workers is a difficult task, however. Many numbers are vague or open to dispute. A few experts contend that the gains are not clear-cut and that any benefits are far from being universally shared.

Special interests that benefit from immigrant labor—including agribusiness, restaurant operators and unions courting new members—tout their gains as gains for all, said Michael Teitelbaum, who was vice chairman of the bipartisan U.S. Commission on Immigration Reform in the 1990s.

"It all comes down to where you sit," said Teitelbaum, a demographer at the Alfred P. Sloan Foundation. "The upper tiers benefit from immigration, and the lower tiers lose."

The 500 economists concede that a "small percentage" of native-born Americans may be hurt by competition from illegal immigrants who are willing to work cheaply. But any harm, they say, is outweighed by the benefits to the overall economy.

Lopez is a case in point. Start with his willingness to work for little. Add his eagerness to spend. Multiply that by the more than 2 million illegal workers in the state.

One result: Restaurant prices are pushed down by illegal labor in the kitchen, fruit and vegetable prices by illegal field hands, new-home prices by illegal drywallers.

Immigrants aren't just a weapon against inflation. The tens of thousands of illegal nannies in the Los Angeles area, for example, lower the cost of child care, freeing mothers to return to work. This in turn increases families' incomes, which encourages spending and fuels the economy.

Many immigrants send a portion of their earnings home to their families, but their influence here remains potent. The Economic Roundtable, a Los Angeles think tank, estimates that the 400,000 illegal workers in L.A. County spend $5.7 billion annually on food, rent, transportation and other necessities.

The sales taxes they pay on all those consumer purchases boost the state treasury. The growing number of immigrants who use false papers to get payroll jobs are contributing to Social Security without the right to receive payments from the fund.

That props up the beleaguered system by at least $5 billion a year, analysts say.

Other benefits may be less obvious, such as the gains in property values enjoyed by homeowners.

Prices surged for a number of reasons over the last few years, including very low interest rates, but experts say immigrants made a big difference in California. Their apartments and houses may be shabby, but their sheer numbers exert a profound effect. In a state that never has enough housing, the hundreds of thousands of units rented to immigrant families put upward pressure on all prices.

> Many Californians . . . [say] immigrants have dragged down the quality of life in the state.

Then there are the bad things that aren't happening despite the immigrants' presence. For instance, they don't seem to be creating an unemployment problem. Joblessness in California, with 24% of the country's illegal immigrants, has tracked the low national rate.

All this evidence, many economists say, makes a powerful argument that immigrants' role can be characterized as somewhere between important and irreplaceable.

"The only people to benefit from the deportation of millions of low-skill workers would be other low-skill workers, who would get an immediate increase in pay rates," said Timothy Kane, an economist with the conservative Heritage Foundation. "However, they would also be the first to lose their jobs during a recession—which would be inevitable if the economy were shocked in this fashion."

Many Californians forcefully disagree with this assessment, saying immigrants have dragged down the quality of life in the state. They point to neighborhoods overflowing with poor immigrants. In some occupations, such as landscaping and construction, workers who don't speak Spanish say they can't get hired.

Other costs carry a more defined price tag. The California Hospital Assn. says emergency-room care for uninsured immigrants, including delivery of babies, costs taxpayers and private insurers about $650 million a year.

Whether born here or brought here, children of illegal immigrants have access to a free education. The Palo Alto–based Center for the Continuing Study of the California Economy estimates that this schooling costs as much as $6 billion annually.

Teitelbaum says the cost is even higher if you take into account how the influx has strained classrooms.

"California used to have one of the best systems of public education," he said. "Now it has one of the worst."

Feeling Squeezed Out

Sean Jourdan stood on the sidewalk at an Inglewood shopping center, hawking DirecTV satellite subscriptions. A natural salesman, he charmed passers-by into taking his bright yellow leaflets.

"Let me give you a flier," he said to a woman and her grandson coming out of the Giant Dollar Store. "What do you have at home? Comcast? I'll give you double what they're giving you for half of what you're paying."

Jourdan took classes at two community colleges but dropped out before getting a degree. When he was in his early 20s, he attended the Maxine Waters Employment Preparation Center in Watts, a school started after the 1965 riots. Trained as a telecommunications technician, he was soon making $50,000 a year installing TV systems.

"It was a living wage," said Jourdan, 32, who is African American. "There are a lot of jobs out there, but only a few pay a living wage."

At first, many of his co-workers were black. Over time, however, his firm reduced payments for installation. Meanwhile, it hired more Latinos. Many couldn't speak English, Jourdan said, so he assumed they were new arrivals from Mexico and Central America.

By the time Jourdan left his last installation job in June, the pay rate for each house call had shrunk so much that he was making only about $25,000 a year. The last company he worked for had two black technicians out of about 25, he said.

Jourdan was briefly in the media spotlight a few months ago after attending a rally for the Minuteman Project, which vehemently opposes illegal immigration. "They're the same type of people who hunted us down when we escaped from the plantation," he said. "But on this issue, I unite with them."

Jourdan grew up near this mall, but it's no longer the place he knew. There's a machine that makes fresh tortillas in the Superior supermarket, signs in Spanish in the Rite Aid and a Latino construction crew redoing a vacant storefront.

"Give me a call. I'll save you money," he promised a young Latina. She smiled and took the flier. Jourdan may be upset by illegal immigrants, but many make good customers because they "haven't had 25 years to run up their credit." Every sale that survives DirecTV's credit check nets Jourdan a $150 commission.

"Although I can make money, it's a hustle," he said. "I'm going to have to learn Spanish."

Workers on the margins can be hurt by illegal immigration, economists note. A 2005 study by Harvard economist George Borjas and Lawrence F. Katz of the National Bureau of Economic Research concluded that native-born high school dropouts lost as much as 8% in wages from 1980 to 2000 because of illegal immigration.

UC Berkeley economist David Card has challenged those findings, saying cities such as Los Angeles are absorbing large numbers of laborers without wages being affected.

The plentiful supply of workers, Card speculates, has led companies to keep people at jobs that might otherwise have been automated.

Other economists wonder whether the reason for the limited effect on wages is even more basic: Instead of competing with immigrants, many native workers simply surrender, perhaps relocating to cities with better prospects.

In a new book titled "L.A. Story: Immigrant Workers and the Future of the U.S. Labor Movement," UCLA sociologist Ruth Milkman uses census data to show how some jobs have changed over the decades.

From 1970 to 2000, Milkman calculates, the percentage of janitors in Greater Los Angeles who were black fell from 24% to 5.2%. Meanwhile, the foreign-born Latino share rose from 10.3% to 63.4%.

Similar transitions occurred among construction drywallers, truckers and garment workers.

As in satellite TV installation, wages for these jobs are a far cry from what they once were. But Milkman says that's not because the companies replaced the natives with illegal workers.

Immigrants, far from being pliant, have reinvigorated the union movement and in some cases won higher wages.

Instead, the employers first squeezed benefits and salaries under the mantle of "competitiveness." The lengthy decline of trade unions undermined workers' ability to fight back.

Natives who could get out did so. The gaps were typically filled by immigrants, but in Milkman's analysis their hiring was a consequence, rather than a cause, of the jobs' lost allure.

The surprising development is that the immigrants, far from being pliant, have reinvigorated the union movement and in some cases won higher wages. "The people who have been demonized, the illegal immigrants, are in some ways showing the way forward for everyone," Milkman said.

For Jourdan, precisely what happened to his installation wages is of little consequence. What matters is the constant worry about slipping behind.

"As a technician, you knew that if you went in every morning and did the work, there'd be a check at the end of the week," he said. "Now I don't have that security."

He's thinking of moving—maybe north to Palmdale or east to Moreno Valley. That's what some of his Inglewood friends have done.

"There are so many homes being built out there, so many potential customers for satellite systems," he said. "Maybe I should go too."

A Region Revitalized

When Panorama City in the San Fernando Valley boomed after World War II, the developers allowed only white people to buy houses. For four decades, General Motors made Chevrolets there, offering at peak production a solid income to more than 5,000 workers.

In 1992, the plant, the Southland's last car factory, was closed. With unemployment in the county running at 10%, few of the assembly-line workers were able to find new jobs paying them the $17 and $18 an hour they had been earning.

Similar closures happened throughout the country. But when the plants shut down in Ohio or Pennsylvania, they tended to become permanent ruins. The surrounding streets festered with abandoned houses and empty storefronts. Pittsburgh, Detroit and Cleveland have had to grapple with massive, long-term population declines.

In Panorama City, vitality quickly reemerged in a new language and a new culture. What it had—which the cities back East lacked—was the proximity of Mexico.

In the 1990s, L.A. County gained 1 million immigrants, most of them from Latin America, many of them illegal. In Panorama City, the Latino population grew from a significant minority to an outright majority.

The community around the former GM plant is thriving, if not exactly upscale. The plant itself is a shopping center called, straightforwardly enough, the Plant. It is anchored by a Home Depot where illegal immigrants wait for work that will pay about half what the autoworkers got, with no benefits and no promises about tomorrow.

On the surrounding streets are clinics, cheap restaurants and music and furniture stores catering to Latinos. It's one of many centers of the informal economy in L.A., where most transactions are in cash.

To many Californians, this is not a change for the better.

"I really don't consider the low-income parts of California to even be California anymore," said Kevin Waterson, an administrative employee of UC Davis, near Sacramento. "The quality of life is much more like that in Mexico."

A year ago, the Public Policy Institute of California polled state residents on whether immigrants were "a burden to California because they use public services" or "a benefit to California because of their hard work and job skills."

"Benefit" was picked by 56% and "burden" by 36%. Many of those in the latter camp, including Waterson, see illegal immigrants as competition. The struggle is less about jobs than scarce community resources, including affordable homes, gridlock-free roads and good schools.

Waterson grew up in Fontana in San Bernardino County, the son of a computer programmer and a billing clerk who were able to buy a three-bedroom house, own two cars and build a nest egg. That status, achieved by millions of Californians after World War II, now feels out of reach.

> If illegal laborers weren't in such demand, they wouldn't risk so much to come here.

"There are a lot of places in Los Angeles I want to live that I can't afford," said Waterson, 27. "The places I can afford, I don't want to live."

It's not just his perception. The Brookings Institution recently found that Los Angeles was the nation's most polarized city by wealth. Fewer than a third of L.A. neighborhoods are middle class, according to its study. The rest are either rich or poor.

Waterson keeps looking for all those benefits the economists say immigration has brought to him. But if the informal economy benefits both the immigrants and the well off, it doesn't seem to be helping him and his wife, Julia, very much.

They don't use immigrants to mow the lawn or wash the car or take care of the kids. They can't afford to eat out, so they don't gain from the toil of illegal restaurant workers. They're renters, so any immigrant-driven boost to real estate just puts a home of their own further out of reach.

The informal economy that much of California has embraced so enthusiastically can be criticized on other grounds.

Small cash-and-carry shops and vendors who cater to immigrants may not pay sales taxes to the state or business license fees to local government. People who hire day laborers cheat the state by not using companies that pay payroll taxes. The laborers cheat the state by not paying income taxes. All of these groups put legal workers and legal businesses at an unfair competitive disadvantage.

The most sweeping criticism: By creating a market for illegal labor, the informal economy increases the supply. If illegal laborers weren't in such demand, they wouldn't risk so much to come here. For better or worse, immigration would not be an issue.

But for Los Angeles County, the informal economy has been better than nothing—and nothing, urban affairs expert and Economic Roundtable President Daniel Flaming says, is what the county would have had otherwise.

"When manufacturing collapsed, there was no effort to salvage the infrastructure for other purposes," he said. "The formal economy here has been stagnant since the beginning of the 1990s. The only growth has been in under-the-table employment, predominantly fueled by desperate workers and in particular undocumented workers."

Without immigrants, Flaming said, Los Angeles would be smaller and weaker and poorer—Detroit or Pittsburgh or Cleveland with better weather.

In that L.A., Waterson would be able to find an affordable house. But because the population might be falling, his house could very well decline in value.

"We should be thankful to immigrants," Flaming said. "Without them, things would be much worse."

First the newcomers stabilized Panorama City. Now they are pushing it forward. The median value of a single-family home has doubled since 2000. And on the edge of the Plant mall, there's a sign that the informal economy might be yielding to a more traditional, bigger-budget state of affairs. Starbucks, that dispenser of $4 venti tangerine frappuccinos to the middle class, has just opened a store.

History of Ambivalence

Five days a week, Lissette Rodriguez starts work at 6 a.m., preparing banquet food for a mid-priced hotel southeast of downtown. After eight hours of chopping and slicing, she goes home and takes a shower. Four days a week, she heads to Beverly Hills, where she works from 5 p.m. to 1 a.m. washing dishes at a luxury hotel.

"Not many people could make it through 16 hours like that," she said proudly.

Rodriguez, 32, arrived from El Salvador in 2004, not to save or damage L.A.'s economy but to help herself.

"In Salvador, there's no money, no jobs," she said in Spanish. "It's more expensive here, but I can make a lot more."

That would be $9 an hour, a fortune to her and a pittance to the hotels. The fact that both sides consider it a good deal binds them together in a "don't ask, don't tell" policy. Rodriguez's employers no more want to catch her than she wants to be exposed.

The history of California is full of ambivalence to immigrants.

"From 1907 to 1940, 'the Mexican problem' was a hardy perennial in Southern California," historian Carey McWilliams wrote in 1946. "Every winter, the business interests of the region worked themselves into a lather of excitement over the cost of Mexican relief, hospitalization and medical care. With the return of the crop cycle in the spring, however, 'the Mexican problem' always somehow vanished or was succeeded by the problem of 'an acute labor shortage.'"

For most employers, any ambivalence appears to be gone. Instead, the business community speaks in dire terms about the consequences of a widespread crackdown on the hiring of illegal workers.

"It would be a horrible negative," said Jeff King, co-founder of King's Seafood Co., which owns Ocean Avenue Seafood in Santa Monica and the Water Grill downtown. "You cannot get Americans to come in at entry-level wages. You'd have to pay a premium."

That might be good for the workers, but King contends it would bring on economic disaster. Prices would go up. Diners would balk. Sales taxes would fall, employment tumble. (King stressed that the 2,000 King's Seafood employees are all legal, as far as the company can tell.)

By working for less than a native citizen would, Lissette Rodriguez is helping her employers' bottom lines.

To an extent, she's also helping taxpayers, although unintentionally. The hotels deduct the usual taxes from her payroll checks. But she won't see a refund or, later in life, a Social Security check.

"That money is just gone," she said. "Most illegals are scared to do tax returns."

Rodriguez is the admirable and problematic face of immigration in 2006. She crossed the border without permission and obtained a bogus Social Security number. She knows she is breaking the law.

Yet she wants only to do what legal immigrants have done throughout U.S. history: work hard and sacrifice mightily to get ahead. In less than two years, she has become deeply embedded in the local economy and the community.

All of these contradictions in one person. All of them in 12 million people. And more tomorrow.

"I miss my children," Rodriguez said. She wants to bring them—a 6-year-old girl, a 15-year-old boy—to Los Angeles. This is her home.

My Life as an Illegal

BY JOHN SPONG
TEXAS MONTHLY, JULY 2006

The word we use with ourselves is mojado. It means "wetback." Or inmigrante ilegal. "Illegal immigrant." But usually we say "wetback." I don't think that's bad or good. That's what they used to call the people a long time ago who used to cross the river. I know those old people, ones who used to come to work here every year, for six months or seven months, and then go hack. I even know some guys who are still doing it, old guys, every year. But I've been here for sixteen years now, since I was sixteen years old, and I have been illegal the whole time.

It has helped that I speak good English. When I got here, I knew words like "table" and "chicken," stuff like that, but when there was no chicken on the table, I was in trouble. You have to learn English if you want to communicate, to earn more money. I went to school, but not to learn English, Maybe I learned it watching TV, reading newspapers.

It also helped that I'm guero. I have clear skin and green eyes, like my four brothers. That's because my dad, who worked as a laborer in our village near Guadalajara until he retired, has green eyes. I think he has some Spanish in him. And my mom, who used to own a restaurant, I guess she's pura mexicana, but she has clear skin. Now, even my wife calls me güero.

My wife is illegal too, and we have been living in Austin for thirteen years. She thinks I'm okay here because I look white, but she gets scared that she might get sent back. She's got darker skin and her English is not as good and she's afraid the migra is going to catch her. There were some rumors a couple weeks ago about Immigration being in stores watching people, like at the H-E-B near our house. So for those days, it was me going to the grocery store because I was scared that something would happen to her. We have three kids who were all born here, who are all American citizens. Even if my wife and I are illegal, they have a right to be here. But if she gets thrown out, who's going to be with the kids? Who's going to be with me?

So we have to watch out, keep an eye out. And we have always tried to do everything right. I pay Social Security tax every week, and I pay income tax every year. I have a driver's license, and I

---

always drive with insurance, inspection, and registration. I don't want to do anything but to become legal and to work and to stay here with my kids. So I do everything right. That's all I want.

I first came to America when I was nine years old. My older brothers brought me to Los Angeles to go to school. Total, we are five brothers and five sisters, and three of my brothers and one sister are here. They all got amnesty in 1986, so everybody here is legal but me.

That first time I used one of my nephews' birth certificates to get across. I was just a kid, so they didn't ask me any questions or anything at the border. They just said, "Come on." I went to junior high in Los Angeles for a year or a year and a half, but things weren't really good. There were family problems, like always. I was not getting along with my brothers, and there were hard times, like no money for rent, things like that. So I went back to Mexico, and that's when I hung out there for five years.

> Everybody wants to come to America. They think it's like you pick up the money with shovels here, which is not true.

When you're in Mexico like I was, it's always nice when you hear about somebody here. You always want to be here. First of all, you hear that you make money, that you wear nice clothes, have nice shoes. Back there, there's nothing. You see, when guys go from America back to Mexico, they always have big, nice trucks. It's hard to buy those back there. So everybody wants to come to America. They think it's like you pick up the money with shovels here, which is not true. You have to work hard for it.

So I came back when I was sixteen to work. I had been living with my parents and depending on them, and I was ready not to depend on anyone anymore. At that time, what you did was ride a bus to Tijuana, and once you were there, you would ask around for a coyote. Everybody knows a coyote, somebody who can get people across. But you have got to know the right guy, because there are some coyotes that can screw you. They take your money and don't pick you up, or they leave you someplace bad. I paid $300 to a guy to show me where to go.

I was with a group of men, and for us, there was no river or anything. We just jumped a six-foot-tall fence and ran across a big field. Then we hid under the trees for, like, ten minutes until somebody said run again. Then we crossed a highway, twelve lanes, and after that, somebody else picked us up and took us to a house somewhere in San Diego. They kept us there in the house for, like, a day. That night there were at least fifty of us, all over the house. We were from all over Mexico or South America. Those people were all strangers, but none of them worried me, because I knew everybody in there had family over here waiting for them and that we all just wanted to make it across and start working.

A van came and got some of us a little bit at a time. We all had to hide in the van. You have to sit on the floor in a line so your back is against the chest of the guy behind you, and somebody else's back is against your chest in front of you. And you have your legs bent so that your knees are by the shoulders of the guy in front of you. You sit like that from San Diego all the way to L.A., so once you get to L.A., your legs are numb. You can barely move. That's where they catch people, because they can't run.

When my family picked me up in L.A., they paid $300 more, and then I went to live with one of my brothers. At first I went to school, but it was just a bunch of gangsters there. Most of them were legal, born and raised in East L.A. I tried to stay away from all that. My parents had told me not to be a gangster, because everybody thinks they're on drugs and because they're always doing something wrong. And I don't like the way those guys dress and the way they lead their lives, always being against something. I always wanted to have a family, and I think a gang's not going to take me anywhere but to jail.

One of my brothers was a foreman with a construction company, and I started working with him, making about $6 or $7 an hour. I needed a Social Security number, and in California, there were a bunch of places where you could get one. I went to a place called Huntington Park, a neighborhood where you could get just about anything: Social Security cards, passports, maybe even birth certificates. There is a Hispanic community there, and they sell them just like selling bread or anything. You say you need a card, and then they deal with you on how much you pay. Sometimes $50, sometimes $100. Then they say, "You just wait here, and in fifteen minutes you will be legal." So I got a fake Social Security number, and it is the same one I have been using ever since.

But things still were not great living with my brother, and I started thinking I might have to move back to Mexico. But I had one sister living in Austin, and she asked me to move here before I went back again. She said to try Texas. I liked it here and stayed.

I married my wife right after I came to Texas. I met Maria (all names in this story have been changed) in Guadalajara when we were both thirteen. It was at my aunt's birthday party, and we started dating on and off. Then, when I was in Texas, she got a visa to come to LA, so I went back and we got married at the courthouse by a judge. He didn't ask questions like "Are you legal?" It was just, "Do you want to get married?" That's all they want.

Before we got married, Maria worked in LA for a company that made bulletproof vests for six and a half months. But when I brought her to Austin, she didn't get a job. At first we lived with my sister, and Maria babysat my sister's daughter. Then she took care of our own kids when we started having them. We had our first child a year after we got here, in 1993. The government paid for everything. She knew she was pregnant right away and started going to a clinic at two months. She filled out a form for Medicaid, which you can get as an illegal. They started giving her vitamins and saying,

"You have to be here at this time so we can check you out." Then my first child was born right here at Brackenridge Hospital, just like my other two children.

At the time, I was working in restaurants as a busboy, a food prep, a cook, and then a manager, at an Indian food place, a hamburger place, a barbecue place, and then a big restaurant, where I ran everything. I made the food orders and the work schedules. I always had two jobs at a time, eight hours in the day at one and then five more hours at night at another, almost every day. When my wife had the kids, I only had one morning off and another afternoon off to see them. It was hard, but you have to work if you want to pay the rent I was only twenty years old, but I had to pay $600 a month for our apartment and $200 a month for our car. And I always send $100 a month home to my parents.

But I needed a job that gave me better money and more time with my family. I had always been like a handyman, done a little bit of everything, and I started doing work for somebody here in town that needed a handyman. He referred me to the guy I work for now, Brian, and I started doing electrical work. That was eight years ago. I'd changed a switch before, but never big jobs like wiring a whole house myself. But I picked it up real fast, in, like, six months, and in about one year of working with Brian, I was also doing side jobs on my own. Somebody would ask me to do something for them and I would do it.

When I started working for Brian, I was still doing part-time in a restaurant. I'd work for Brian from eight until two and then go from four until close in a restaurant. Then Brian asked if I would work for him fulltime. He said, "I hate it when you go to work over there and I still have work here. So how much you want for staying here?" I told him the only reason I was working at the restaurant was because if there was any rain and he didn't need me, I would still always have work and a free meal at the restaurant. So he said he would give me forty hours a week no matter what, and now I've been with him eight years.

Eventually I needed to get an electrician's license. I went to a class to know the codes, but there was a program that they called "grandfathering." I had been doing electrician work for eight years, and they said, "If you have that much experience, we will just give you a license." So I showed them my Social Security card and that was it.

That's the same number Brian uses for my withholding on my paycheck. But I have a taxpayer ID number that I use to pay income tax. I got it at the Social Security office in North Austin. I just filled out the form, and they gave it to me. It's made for people who are not U.S. citizens so you don't use someone else's number. I turn both numbers in with my taxes, the fake one and the real one, but they only look at the real one. And I don't worry about them seeing the fake one and coming looking for me because Social Security doesn't have anything to do with immigration. Nothing.

Some guys that are here illegally don't want to do all this because they are afraid something bad is going to happen. But if somebody says, "Have you been doing your taxes?" we want to be able to show them we have. And I do it also because they send you money back. My refund this year was $3,500.

We're always aware that we don't have a legal card, so we do all of these things to stay out of trouble, but also to lead a normal life. We take the kids to church every Sunday, because that's the way we grew up. The kids like school, and we go with them when they are in a show or make a presentation. We just try to live normal.

The people where I'm from in Mexico who move to America all go to Indianapolis. One of my godfathers has been there for years, and he said that the first time he came to America, he went all the way there because he heard there was a lot of work. He says now that if you see somebody Hispanic in the street in Indianapolis they are from our hometown. I've been there and it's a nice place, but I don't know why they like it. It's cold in the winter. I call them and they tell me how many inches of snow there are or that it's 5 degrees out. I like Texas.

We're always aware that we don't have a legal card,
so we do all of these things to stay out of trouble,
but also to lead a normal life.

I went back to visit my little town in Mexico more often when I was single. But since I got married I have only been twice. The last time I went was the winter before 9/11 happened. It was easy then. When I was coming back, I just walked across the border and said I was a U.S. citizen and they let me back in. But I decided it's not a good idea for me to go anymore. Basically, I am the support of my family, and I need to work and pay bills, and I am afraid maybe I couldn't get back across or I could be put in jail.

Maria took the kids to try to live in Mexico a few years ago to see how it would work, just in case something happens. They didn't like it. Maria said the schools were not good. There were fifty kids in a classroom with one teacher, and first graders and sixth graders were going outside to play at the same time. The smaller kids were being picked on.

And I don't think there were any schools there for my son. He has special needs. He's smart, but he has speech problems. He does not communicate all that well. So he's in a special program here. And even though my wife and I speak Spanish, he speaks it very little. He speaks much more English. If you ask if he wants to go back to Mexico, he will say no and start crying.

We don't really have a plan if one of us gets deported except to come back as quick as we can. When I lived with my sister, I saw other illegal leave money with somebody they knew well, like a cousin or a friend, somebody who you know is not going to spend it. Leave, like, $1,000 or $2,000 and say, "If something happens, just send this down to me in Mexico." Then the friend would send a MoneyGram from the Money Box store and sometimes it would go to a bank or sometimes you would pick it up. And then you would be back here in a week.

My wife and I have each other for that. And I tell her to keep some money in her wallet to get a hotel or to eat in case she gets thrown out and then just try to get back. If she cannot, I'll send the kids to her and stay here and work. But we don't want to do that. That's something we don't like to think about, really. It's depressing.

There is a guy on one of Austin's all-Spanish radio stations who everybody listens to called El Chulo. That's where we hear a lot about the immigration protests. Chulo is on early in the morning, from five-thirty to ten, and I hear him when I'm at work. It's like a talk show, not much music, and it's also on in Dallas and San Antonio.

May 1 was Mexican Labor Day, and there was a protest in Austin that day. For that protest, Chulo was telling us, "Don't go to work. Don't do this, don't do that. Don't buy food at McDonald's or Jack in the Box, nothing. Stay home. Don't watch TV. Don't do anything that day." That's how he is. He always talks about real life. Some guys don't like him because he talks about sex a lot and girls call in and he flirts with them. But sometimes people call in with crazy stories, like about girls being raped by the Border Patrol or about people coming from Mexico and having all their money taken away. Every day there is a subject, like immigration or coyotes. He helps people. When Immigration was here after the protest, some guys called and said the migra was at H-E-B. Chulo told us about it and said not to go there.

I heard there were a lot of raids in Austin after the protest, but I didn't see them. I was at work one Monday morning, and I went to lunch, and when I got back, some guy said, "Hey, Immigration came by." Everybody had run away. Some of the guys were from San Antonio, and they got all their stuff and left and never came back to the job. But I don't know anybody close to me who was deported, and I have many close friends who work construction. So maybe it happened, but who knows? Even if it did, I think the protests were good. Everybody wants to get legal somehow, so we do this protest in as nice and positive a way as we can.

My kids don't know we are illegal. Sometimes kids talk to other kids at school, and the other kids talk to their parents. We try not to tell everybody that we're not legal because you never know. Like my neighbor here, he doesn't know. He always talks about wetbacks, and he doesn't know he's got one next door.

So we just tell the kids that we don't have passports. Maria took two of them with her to a protest in Austin before the Labor Day protest, and they asked her why they were going. She told them everyone was going because they wanted to get papers. When it was over, they asked her, "Mom, why didn't you get your papers?" She said, "Maybe it will take a little longer. Maybe a few more protests. Maybe we'll have to walk to Washington."

I couldn't go because I was busy with work. And I didn't want her to go. But she said she wanted to go because it is an important time. And when it was finished, she said she felt like she had freed herself.

> There's a lot of people that don't like us to be here, but the thing is, we are here.

Everybody was there together, feeling the same way as her, whether they were illegal or American citizens trying to do something to help somebody else.

I want to start by being a legal resident, and then I'd like to be a U.S. citizen. They could change the law like that. You start with a permit to work, and then if you don't get in any trouble, they give you the citizenship to stay here and go in and out of America legally. Maybe after eighteen years of the permit, you could get citizenship.

I know they have a test you take now. You have to learn to read and write English good to pass the test. Some guys tell me it's hard, but sometimes they just don't know much. One guy told me that they ask how many states America has and what are the colors of the flag. And they ask you to write something in English. That guy failed the test because he couldn't write the word "yellow," which is funny, because he is a painter.

There's a lot of people that don't like us to be here, but the thing is, we are here. Those people might be mad with guys doing something wrong, like bringing drugs. I agree with them on that. It's okay to be mad at those dudes, but don't be mad at everybody. It's like the way they look at everybody who has brown skin and is dressed like a cowboy and say, "He must be a Mexican," even if the guy is from El Salvador. We can tell somebody's not from Mexico by the way they talk, by their face. But here everybody thinks, "That's a Mexican."

I heard about the three-year guest-worker program. That has been on the news a lot. I think I would like to do that because it's the first step to be legal. But I need to see what's going to happen after three years. If you have to leave after that, then no, I don't think that will work for me. Three years go fast.

I could go talk to an attorney, but sometimes you are afraid to do that. Nobody is looking for us right now. But if we start getting into this process and they look for more information, that might be when they say, "Okay, here they are," and then we get deported.

I want to be legal. I want to buy a house, like a bigger house with more rooms. But because we are illegal, they would ask for too much interest on it. And I would like to be able to take my kids home to see where I grew up and maybe see my old friends. We are not far from Guadalajara. It is only a sixteen-hour drive. I would like to be able to get in our own car and drive there for a couple weeks and then come back.

I guess there's hope when my son turns 21. Then he can apply for citizenship for me. It's too late for me to do like some guys who get married to a U.S. citizen, because I'm already married. Who knows, maybe I'll win the lottery. I bet they would give me citizenship then.

But until then we will just keep doing everything right and waiting.

Divided over Immigration

By Jennifer Delson
HISPANIC, October 2005

Andy Ramírez, the grandson of Mexican immigrants, chose to celebrate Mexican Independence Day on the border this year. The fiesta did not include the traditional parade or *grito*, the ceremonial call to independence that usually caps the day.

Instead, on the sun-baked edge of California, Ramírez chose to spend the holiday on September 16 with binoculars in hand. He planned to look for illegal immigrants crossing into the United States. With several hundred supporters who call themselves Friends of the Border Patrol, he has conceived what he hopes to be an indefinite citizen patrol designed to demonstrate the failed immigration policies in the United States.

"Detractors say we are traitors, or coconuts," says Ramírez, who chose Mexican Independence Day to highlight the effort that is similar to the Minuteman campaign in April in Arizona. "We need to show people that there are Latinos who want to stand up for the law. We want to support what is right."

Variety of Views

The participation of Ramírez and other Latinos in the anti-immigrant movement remains atypical, but nonetheless stands as a reminder of how Hispanics around the country are taking a variety of roles in the ever louder debate about immigration.

Gov. Bill Richardson, who is Hispanic, recently declared a state of emergency in New Mexico, citing deleterious effects of illegal immigrants pouring through.

Meanwhile, leaders of the League of United Latin American Citizens in Houston protested comments made by House Majority Leader Tom DeLay, who told Indiana Republicans that he does not support educating illegal immigrants or having their U.S.–born children automatically become citizens.

In Tucson, Arizona, Isabel García, who heads the immigrant advocate group, Derechos Humanos, has countered the citizen border patrols in her state with vigils and talks to educate listeners about immigrants and their needs.

As tensions rise, the Pew Hispanic Center released in August a survey generating debate and discussion about the plethora of opinions Hispanics hold about illegal immigration.

The survey's results debunk any idea that the Hispanic community is the monolith it was once perceived to be. Opinions vary depending on country of origin, social class and education levels. Differing views may surge regionally based on personal experience with immigrants.

"There is a political pluralism in the community," says Harry Pachón, president of the Tomás Rivera Policy Institute. "As you get second, third and four generations, it's not unusual that there will be varying opinions."

The Pew study showed the majority of U.S. Latinos oppose granting driver's licenses to undocumented residents, but favor granting illegal aliens permanent legal status and eventual citizenship.

Seventy-six percent of foreign-born Latinos said undocumented residents helped the economy by providing cheap labor but among U.S. born Latinos, the number was 20 percentage points lower.

The U.S. economy uses the labor of illegal immigrants, but only selectively enforces federal law that prohibits them from working here.

Fifty-six percent of Latinos prefer a temporary worker program that would allow undocumented immigrants, currently estimated at 11 million people, to live and work in the United States before returning home. Eighty-four percent favor proposals that would give undocumented immigrants permanent legal status and allow them to become citizens. The split among Hispanics is not just present in large cities but has fanned out to small hamlets throughout the United States, many of which now have sizable immigrant populations.

A New Activism

The U.S. economy uses the labor of illegal immigrants, but only selectively enforces federal law that prohibits them from working here. In certain regions, particular economic sectors rely on immigrant labor, so much that in some cases employers lobby the government to find them visas. Yet paying for health care, education and impacts on local infrastructure is a burden taxpayers shoulder. The contradiction leads to activism in new frontiers.

Local police arrested illegal immigrants for trespassing in New Hampshire and activists rallied against illegal immigrants in Tennessee. On the radio, many AM talk radio hosts spend part of the day taking calls about illegal immigrants.

What surprises some is seeing Hispanics like Ramírez as leaders in the anti-immigrant movement. They are few and far between, but nonetheless gaining attention in places like Illinois and Idaho because they are Hispanic and they attract applause from members of anti-immigrant groups who seek to defuse criticism that they are racists.

Many supporting the anti-immigrant movement say that they have grown up in Latino neighborhoods and charge that their communities have been worsened by the influx of Hispanic immigrants.

Ramírez, 37, a one-time professional hockey player disabled by multiple sclerosis, says he began participating in the citizen patrol movement because he had waited hours for medical care in hospitals that treat undocumented immigrants near his home in Chino, California. He believes that people who come to this country illegally consume resources that could improve the lives of legal U.S. residents, including money for health and education.

He has Latino allies, among them, Lupe Moreno, a veteran activist who speaks against illegal immigration pervasive in her hometown of Santa Ana, California.

"Things are heating up," says Moreno of the current tension over illegal immigration. "For the first time, Latinos are coming out of the woodwork to support us."

In Idaho, Canyon County Commissioner Robert Vásquez, whose grandfather emigrated from Mexico, authored a resolution to make his county a federal emergency area because he says an influx of illegal immigrants jeopardizes local funding of indigent medical care and incarceration.

Rosana Pulido of Chicago, the 49-year-old grandchild of Mexican immigrants, spent four days with the Minuteman patrol in Arizona and is now organizing Latino activists to fight illegal immigration in her city.

Mixed Feelings

Ian Haney López, a University of California Berkeley law professor, says Latinos have long held mixed feelings about immigration. Some Latinos feel pulled between two identities, he says. When there is a strong desire to be American, some Latinos cast aside everything from their country of origin.

From that perspective, "what jeopardizes Hispanics is the continuing influx of immigrants," says López. "They are on the street corners. They tend to be dark, poor and uneducated. That brings down the status of the group."

Pablo Alvarado, 38, who has spent three years as the coordinator of the National Day Laborer Organizing Network, says he believes that polls such as the Pew Center's show how a media frenzy has created misunderstandings about immigration that even permeate the Latino community.

Immigrants should not be demonized because that foments hatred and racism, he argues. Instead, the problem should be viewed as one of supply and demand in the labor market, he says.

"What is happening shows a great deal of ignorance about immigration and the forces behind it, says Alvarado, a one-time Salvadoran farmworker who was recently named one of the 25 most influential Hispanics in the United States by *Time*, as well as "the New Cesar Chávez."

In Tucson, Isabel García says she is equally frustrated by the emphasis on the immigrants, instead of inhumane immigration policy. Jobs are freely given to immigrants, provided they can get through a potentially fatal and illegal trip through the desert. The North American Free Trade Agreement has hurt Mexico's economy and lessened job opportunities in Mexico, which in turn has made El Norte more attractive, she says.

"The reality is that this country has always relied on immigrants," García says. "We need them more than ever. Why are there people promoting the misconception that people who walk 1,000 miles have come not for a job but for welfare?"

A Complex Community

And yet although most Hispanics are immigrants, related to immigrants or personally know immigrants, there are some whose experience does not make them sympathetic.

Moreno's family home had served as a safe house for undocumented immigrants. Her former husband was an illegal immigrant. And in part, it is her guilt that has driven her to participate—but not on behalf of illegal workers.

She has participated in border watch efforts in California and Arizona, as well as in rallies, such as a July event at a day laborer site in Laguna Beach. She has also lobbied in Sacramento against allowing driver's licenses for undocumented immigrants.

"If you are a patriotic Latino American," her website reads, "and you are tired of hearing Latino left-wing activist groups mislead the public by asserting that they represent you with the usual remarks about our country being racist, and that anyone who is against illegal immigration is against immigration, join us in raising our voices for family, truth, God and America."

Some who disagree say that view just shows the complexity inherent in the Hispanic community that spans through 50 states and thousands of miles.

Hispanics are so American that we have a community that includes a wide variety of opinion, says Héctor Flores, who is national president of the League of United Latin American Citizens.

Yet like many who have long fought for the rights of Hispanics, Flores does not have much sympathy for those who support the Minuteman and similar citizen border patrols.

"How can we hold accountable people who are trying to feed their families?" asks Flores, who as a youth worked as a migrant farmworker. "When you have a labor market that needs these people, they come. They help maintain the quality of our lives, of my life. They are people who are making sure those great veggies are on my plate. They are planting them, picking them and cooking them."

III. The Growing Political Clout of Hispanic Americans

Editor's Introduction

For years pundits have predicted that the country's growing Hispanic population will fundamentally reshape the national political landscape. Among these prognosticators, most maintain that the changes wrought by this emerging demographic have thus far aided—and will likely continue to aid—the Democratic Party. The reasoning behind this assumption is fairly simple: The Democratic Party has traditionally attracted the support of immigrant communities and in most modern elections has captured healthy majorities of the Latino vote. In their book *The Emerging Democratic Majority* (2002), Ruy Teixeira and John Judis predict that these trends will continue as the Hispanic population increases in demographic clout and that, consequently, a secure Democratic ruling majority is likely to emerge in the near future.

However, the national election of 2004 suggested that no particular party can count on the Hispanic vote, as initial reports indicated that President George W. Bush had captured a healthy 44 percent share of total Hispanic voters. While this figure was subsequently lowered to around 40 percent, it nevertheless remained an impressive and perhaps decisive showing for the president, who was narrowly reelected, and the Republican Party, which aside from its dominance within the Cuban American community, had generally fared poorly among Latinos as a whole.

In the two years since, however, the Republicans have failed to build on their success: The debate over undocumented workers, coupled with political troubles at home and abroad, has effectively undermined earlier Republican gains. Indeed, in the 2006 congressional elections, Republican support among Hispanics fell to 29 percent, helping Democrats capture both the House of Representatives and the Senate. Thus, for the moment, Hispanic Americans appear to have aligned themselves with the Democratic Party, and consequently—2004 notwithstanding—Teixeira and Judis's thesis might still be operable.

The articles in this chapter chart the growing political influence of Hispanic Americans, emphasizing the issues and personalities that have motivated them over the years as well as their voting patterns in recent elections. The first entry, "A Latin Power Surge," by Arian Campo-Flores and Howard Fineman, examines the impressive victory of Mexican-American Democrat Antonio Villaraigosa in the 2005 Los Angeles mayoral election. During the course of the campaign, Villaraigoa, the first Latino mayor of the city in over 100 years, assembled a vibrant multiethnic coalition that Fineman and Campo-Flores believe not only illustrates how to effectively motivate Hispanic voters, but also offers valuable insight into why Republicans gained and Democrats lost ground in the national elections of 2004.

Despite their recent impact at the polls and the intensity with which their votes are sought by the Republican and Democratic Parties, Hispanics have lower rates of political participation than other groups. Roberto Suro, in the subsequent piece, "Latino Power?" explains why this is so.

Richard Nadler discusses President George W. Bush's surprisingly strong showing among Hispanic voters in the 2004 election in the next entry, "Bush's 'Real' Hispanic Numbers." Nadler breaks down the statistics to determine what factors proved decisive in the president's appeal to the Latino voter.

Unfortunately for Bush, his Republican allies failed to replicate his 2004 success in 2006. In the final piece in this chapter, "G.O.P. Risking Hispanic Votes on Immigration," David D. Kirkpatrick anticipates the Republican electoral debacle by exploring how elements of the Republican Party alienated Latino voters during the immigration debate, thus sabotaging the president's efforts to construct a moderate consensus on the issue.

A Latin Power Surge

By Arian Campo-Flores and Howard Fineman
Newsweek, May 30, 2005

Antonio Villaraigosa's cell phone was trilling incessantly. Every Democrat in the nation, it seemed, wanted a piece of the newly elected mayor of Los Angeles, the first Latino to win the office in 133 years. John Kerry phoned to congratulate him, as did John Edwards, Howard Dean, Al Gore and Sen. Chris Dodd. Driving to city hall last Friday as he spoke by phone with a Newsweek reporter, Villaraigosa interrupted the interview to field yet another call on a different phone. "Yes, I would like to speak to Senator Clinton," he said. "Can I call you back?" he told the reporter. Afterward, Villaraigosa recounted his exchange with Hillary: "She said that she and President Clinton were just elated with my victory," and "if they could be helpful in any way in the coming weeks and months," they were eager to do so. Villaraigosa said he had responded with a few admiring words of his own. She was "an example of what I need to do as mayor of the city of Los Angeles," he had told her. "Not get so caught up in all of the national attention and focus on my job."

Good luck. The stream of calls may well build into a deluge. Dashing and charismatic, with street smarts bred in the barrio, Villaraigosa accomplished what Democrats dream of doing nationwide: he energized Latino voters to turn out for him at historic levels and stitched together the sort of multiracial coalition that has often eluded less-gifted politicians. Though they won the Hispanic vote last November, Democrats lost ground to Republicans for the second straight presidential-election cycle. President George W. Bush captured roughly 40 percent (the exact figure remains in dispute) of the Hispanic vote, compared with 35 percent in 2000 and Bob Dole's 21 percent in 1996. For the Democrats, the set-back came in just the year that Latino voters, long considered a sleeping giant, stirred from their slumber. With turnout increasing from about 6 million in 2000 to an estimated 8 million last year, the Hispanic vote has become the El Dorado of American elections. To remain viable as a party, Democrats need to win Latinos back. At stake is nothing less than control of the presidency and Congress. If the G.O.P. maintains its current share of the Latino vote, says Simon Rosenberg of the New Democrat Network, "then the Democrats will never be the majority party again in our lifetimes."

How did things become so dire for the Democrats? For starters, John Kerry's campaign botched its Hispanic outreach, according to many accounts. Latino operatives complained that the campaign leadership marginalized and undermined them at every turn. The leadership's assumption, according to Paul Rivera, a senior political adviser on the campaign: that Latino votes would break down roughly as they did in 2000, as a Democracy Corps poll last July wrongly suggested. The Hispanic team struggled constantly for resources, the operatives say, and assurances of ad buys in battle-ground states often went unfulfilled, keeping Kerry off the Spanish-language airwaves for days at a time. "If the Kerry campaign had won Nevada, Arizona and New Mexico," all Latino-rich states, says Tom Castro, the campaign's deputy national finance chair, "John Kerry would be president right now."

Over at the Bush-Cheney campaign headquarters, where Latino outreach was embraced zealously, a different world order prevailed. "We were sitting at the big kids' table," says Frank Guerra, a consultant on the national media team. He and Lionel Sosa—a Hispanic marketing guru and veteran of six presidential campaigns—joined weekly conference calls with campaign strategists and chimed in freely with suggestions for Hispanic ads and even general-market ones. A master of the softly lit spot saluting Hispanic heritage and patriotism, Sosa built his ads around a consistent theme: "Nos conocemos" ("We know each other"). As he puts it, "We have a great leader, a man of his word, a man that truly is close to us." But Sosa also cut attack ads, an infrequent tactic in Hispanic political marketing. For one series of spots, he dispatched a cameraman to a Latino neighborhood within miles of Kerry's Beacon Hill home in Boston. "Have you ever seen him here?" the interviewer asked people on the street. "Has he been to any fiesta?" (He hadn't.)

With Karl Rove, a direct-mail devotee, at the helm, Republicans tailored messages to particular segments of the Latino electorate—a strategy they hope will keep winning over converts on the road to 2008. They targeted first-generation Hispanics with Spanish-language ads and second and third-generation Latinos with English-language spots. "The day of advertising simply in Spanish to reach the Hispanic voter is dead," says Guerra. The campaign also tweaked some messages to appeal to particular nationalities clustered in different regions—like Cuban-Americans in Miami or Mexican-Americans in the Southwest—using radio announcers who could summon an array of accents and local idioms. "You don't dare use one accent in the wrong place," says Blaise Underwood, a grass-roots organizer for the campaign.

But the segmentation strategy that most worries Democrats involves religion. As with voters generally, last year the campaign courted Hispanic evangelical Protestants, who make up a growing portion of a traditionally Roman Catholic constituency. "In some states, such as New Mexico," says Underwood, "most of the evangelicals we were targeting were Hispanic." By reaching out to such

churches, the campaign tapped into large concentrations of potentially sympathetic souls. "Many evangelical communities are greatly
identified with the Hispanic community," says Roberto Suro, director of the Pew Hispanic Center. "That explicit ethnic connection is
considerably more rare in the Catholic Church." The Republican
effort reaped rewards. According to a Pew Hispanic study scheduled
for release this week, Bush's support among Latino Protestants—
who comprise one third of the overall Latino electorate—grew from
44 percent in 2000 to 56 percent in 2004. Democrats were caught
flat-footed. They "were so focused on the 527s, I'm not sure . . . they
paid sufficient attention to the 3:16s," says Luis Lugo, director of
the Pew Center on Faith and Public Life, referring to the Biblical
passage from the Gospel of John. Unlike black churchgoers who
remain mostly Democratic for socioeconomic reasons, Lugo says,
Latinos are "not a community in which economic issues alone are
going to win it."

Hispanics had become much more of a swing
constituency than a base [in 2004], and no one
could take their votes for granted anymore.

Out-maneuvered and outspent, the Kerry campaign learned a
definitive lesson on Election Day: Hispanics had become much more
of a swing constituency than a base, and no one could take their
votes for granted anymore. In the aftermath, Kerry's Latino staffers
and advisers, who had warned of such an outcome, vowed never to
let it happen again. On Nov. 23, about 30 Latino Democrats con-
vened in Washington, D.C., to plot strategy for future battles.
Among the results: a proposal to create a new partisan Latino organization—for which $25,000 was quickly raised for a feasibility
study—and a new group called the Coronado Project, composed of
several members of Kerry's Hispanic team. This week the Coronado
group will send a 12-page memo to a variety of Democratic bigwigs
with a caustic critique of the party's handling of Hispanic outreach
and a set of recommendations. "Failure to reform the party's
approach to Latino voters," the memo reads, "maintains a caste system that is ineffective, if not suicidal, for the party." Recently, Kerry
himself acknowledged his campaign's anemic Hispanic effort. During a dinner for Latino backers at his Georgetown home last month,
he offered what two guests called "a full mea culpa" and the assur-
ance that he'd strive to avoid a similar fiasco in the future. (The two
guests asked not to be named because they considered it a private
event.)
   As a party, the Democrats' renewed commitment faces its first test
in the midterm elections next year. On his travels as head of the
Democratic National Committee, Howard Dean is making sure to

schmooze Hispanics along the way—granting a recent interview, for instance, to El Latino, a Spanish-language weekly in Arkansas. The DNC has also run Spanish-language ads as part of its assault on Bush's Social Security plan. And the New Democrat Network, which poured $6 million into a comprehensive program to target first-generation Hispanics during the 2004 cycle, is eyeing potential races to direct resources to next year.

> Republican ardor for Hispanics is as caliente as ever.

Some Latinos see a political opening in Bush's immigration policies—arguing that the president's guest-worker program, for example, does not do nearly enough to help the community that has shown him so much support. For their part, Republican ardor for Hispanics is as caliente as ever. Dean's counterpart at the Republican National Committee, Ken Mehlman, recently formed a Hispanic advisory committee with an impressive cast of luminaries, including George P. Bush, the president's half-Mexican nephew. Mehlman recently addressed the Latin Chamber of Commerce in Las Vegas and has held a "conversation with the community" in Orlando, Fla. Underwood, the G.O.P. grass-roots organizer, says the party will be trying to master the complex brew of Hispanic nationalities in Florida during next year's Senate contest. "President Bush has given Republicans an opportunity," says chief polling strategist Matthew Dowd. "He's tilled the soil among Hispanics. Now we have to work it."

Faced with such G.O.P. incursions, Democrats will be studying Villaraigosa's formula for victory, hoping to replicate it in other races nationwide—where the terrain may be more challenging than two Democrats squaring off in a Left Coast city. Villaraigosa captured 84 percent of an energized Latino-base vote, combined with half the white vote and nearly half the black one. Villaraigosa's "coalition-building is a map to be followed," says U.S. Rep. Luis Gutierrez of Illinois, a Democrat, who hopes to emulate him in a future Chicago mayoral run. To cobble his alliance together, Villaraigosa had to perform an adroit balancing act—galvanizing his Hispanic supporters without coming across as ethnocentric and thereby alienating other racial groups. "He neither played [his ethnicity] nor downplayed it," says Rodolfo de la Garza of Columbia University. "It was just there." Villaraigosa assured he'd be a mayor "for all of Los Angeles," and assiduously courted other groups, most importantly blacks, who voted overwhelmingly for his opponent during their previous face-off in 2001. This time, his efforts paid off: he secured key endorsements from leaders like U.S. Rep. Maxine Waters and former L.A. Lakers star Magic Johnson.

The experiences of Villaraigosa's predecessors offer insights as well. Back when black mayors were sweeping into power in major metropolitan areas, many of them also knit together multiracial coalitions. David Dinkins—New York's first and only African-American mayor, elected in 1989—brought together black, brown and white folks on a foundation of organized labor, recalls Bill Lynch, who helped build the bloc. "If you energize your core base [blacks], it has a contagion effect on the other parts of the coalition," he says. It's what Fernando Ferrer needs to address in his current New York mayoral run if he has any chance of reviving a candidacy hobbled by some controversial remarks he made about the case of Amadou Diallo, who was gunned down by police in 1999. "If the Latino vote is going to count, it needs to be cohesive and establish a strong link to other groups," says de la Garza. "My own sense is that Ferrer is not energizing the base." But Lynch, who's advising Ferrer, says "it's still early in the process."

Increasingly, Latino candidates must confront another barrier: African-American misgivings about a surging Hispanic population. While blacks are accustomed to playing the dominant role in multi-racial coalitions, says Lynch, "what happened in L.A. sends a clear signal that that could be about to change. There's always potential for power struggle in a coalition." Historically, de la Garza argues, blacks have hesitated to share the stage with Latinos. "They initially opposed extending the nomenclature of 'minority' to Latinos in the Voting Rights Act," he says. As much as things have evolved since then, "the romantic image of blacks and browns uniting is just that—romantic."

Which may lead some Latinos to ask: Will there be a day when they can simply rely on their own demographic power to propel candidates into office? In recent years Hispanics have made considerable gains, winning in some unlikely places, such as Wichita, Kansas (mayor), Idaho (state senator) and Carrboro, N.C. (alderman). There are now more than 6,000 Hispanic elected officials, according to the National Association of Latino Elected Officials. Just last year the Senate gained the first two Latinos in recent times: Republican Mel Martinez from Florida and Democrat Ken Salazar from Colorado. Yet in most of these cases, the candidates won because they either resided in majority-minority districts or they fashioned new iterations of multiethnic and multiracial alliances. Even if Latinos were to pursue a singularly Hispanic campaign strategy in a competitive race, their dizzying diversity—with recently arrived Dominicans, Cuban-American exiles and 10th-generation New Mexicans living under one umbrella—would raise its own prickly issues. Whatever the strategy, though, the bottom line is that Latinos are steadily securing higher office. While the traditional critique of Hispanic politics has been "that you guys aren't ready for prime time," says Antonio Gonzalez of the William C. Velasquez Institute, Villaraigosa shows that "Latinos can win the big one." Surely the next victory can't be too far away. Democrats had better pray they're part of it.

Latino Power?

By Roberto Suro
The Washington Post, June 26, 2005

Politicians and the news media seem entranced by Latino voters. The chairmen of both national parties addressed the annual convention of the National Association of Latino Elected Officials, which wrapped up its annual convention in Puerto Rico yesterday. President Bush appeared before the National Hispanic Prayer Breakfast earlier this month, and much of the buzz about the next Supreme Court nomination centers on whether a name with a lot of vowels will get sent up.

Meanwhile the Democratic National Committee has produced a 60-second radio ad in Spanish trying to mobilize Latino voters against Bush's proposed changes in Social Security. "Call your member of Congress and tell him or her not to privatize Social Security and threaten the future of Hispanic retirees and their families," the ad says. The White House, for its part, has dispatched Anna Escobedo Cabral, a Mexican American who is the treasurer of the United States, to tout the administration's Social Security ideas.

All this public wooing, and a good deal of behind-the-scenes strategizing, stems from a simple fact: The number of Latino votes in last November's election jumped 23 percent over those cast in the 2000 balloting. That was more than twice the growth rate for non-Hispanic whites, even though the election was marked by higher-than-normal turnout in a polarized white electorate. Moreover, all the trend lines point to continued growth in the Latino population in the future.

Normally, in an article of this sort, this would be the place to deploy the "sleeping giant" metaphor, hailing the rise of a powerful new voting bloc that's changing the American political landscape. But the Latino population isn't a cliche; it can't be so easily characterized. The rapid increase in its size has not produced a corresponding growth in its political clout—and won't for some time to come.

Consider these contrasting pieces of information. The census report that made headlines a few weeks ago showed that Hispanics (that's the Census Bureau's official term) accounted for half of all the population growth in the United States over the past four years. But another, less heralded, census document showed that Hispanics accounted for only one-tenth of the increase in all votes cast in 2004

---

compared with the 2000 election. The growth of the Latino population as a whole may be gigantic, but only one out of every four Latinos added to the U.S. population is an added voter.

That's why in close elections, politicians tend to focus their ardor on traditional partners—unions, churches, ethnic groups—that have shown they can effectively bring voters to the polls. Cultivating a solid Hispanic constituency will require a lengthy courtship.

> Cultivating a solid Hispanic constituency will require a lengthy courtship.

True, Latinos have made gains in elected positions, but the advances have been relatively modest. Two Hispanic U.S. senators were elected last year, and the number of Hispanics in the House edged up to 27.

But the Latinos who gain national prominence still tend to be the ones who have it bestowed upon them by white political patrons, such as President Bush's Attorney General Alberto Gonzales or President Bill Clinton's cabinet officers Henry Cisneros and Bill Richardson.

There are two reasons why Latino population growth hasn't translated directly into political clout, according to a new report by the Pew Hispanic Center, a nonpartisan research organization where I work.

First, a lot of Latinos aren't U.S. citizens. A third of the Latino population increase between 2000 and 2004 came from an influx of adult immigrants who cannot vote here. Under current law, most never will. About two-thirds of the new arrivals have come here illegally. The rest, who are legal immigrants, are facing backlogs and processing delays that have slowed the pace of naturalizations since 9/11.

The other big source of population increases for Latinos comes from new births. Nearly a third of the Hispanic population growth since 2000 consists of people not eligible to vote because they are under 18 years of age. The vast majority of these individuals are native-born U.S. citizens, but it will be a long time before they are old enough to vote. About 80 percent of them will still be too young in 2008.

The impact of these two demographic factors becomes evident when you compare how black and Hispanic population numbers translate into numbers of voters. In 2004, Hispanics outnumbered blacks by nearly 5 million in the population count, but blacks had nearly 7.5 million more eligible voters. To put it another way, eligible voters made up 39 percent of the Hispanic population compared with 64 percent of blacks.

This demographic calculus calls for some caution when assessing the Latino population's impact on American politics. Last month, when Antonio Villaraigosa became the first Latino mayor of Los Angeles since 1872, commentators rushed to proclaim a new era.

"Latino Power," declared the headline on Newsweek's May 30 cover story, complete with a sleeping giant metaphor. Villaraigosa was credited with generating a record turnout among Latinos, but given the low baseline, it wasn't hard. When it comes to counting people in almost any category, Latinos break their own records every day.

Villaraigosa's victory does not signal the arrival of a new ethnic colossus striding across the political landscape. Rather, it was a measure of widespread voter dissatisfaction with the incumbent, James K. Hahn, and of Villaraigosa's ability to draw votes from a variety of non-Hispanic constituencies. Latinos produced a quarter of the vote, according to Los Angeles Times exit polling. Sure, that was a record and by taking 84 percent of those votes, Villaraigosa helped assure himself of a landslide. But, Hispanics make up half of the city's population. So, even when a popular Latino is running for office in a city where Hispanics are well organized and have elected many representatives to other posts, low numbers of voters cut Latino power in half.

Part of the reason the metaphorical Latino giant is not a bigger player in the political game is because it is still half asleep.

Demographics aren't the only factors diluting the Hispanic presence at the polls. Last year, even though both major political parties, unions and nonpartisan groups all targeted Latinos with voter registration drives, Hispanics failed to fulfill their potential for political participation.

Even among eligible voters, only 58 percent of Latinos were registered last year and that was significantly fewer than either whites (75 percent) or blacks (69 percent). Actual turnout in the 2004 presidential election also was lower for Hispanics than for other groups, albeit by a lesser margin. If Latinos had registered and voted at the same rate as whites of the same age, they would have cast an additional 2.7 million ballots, increasing their tally of 7.6 million votes by 36 percent.

So part of the reason the metaphorical Latino giant is not a bigger player in the political game is because it is still half asleep.

That's why fears among some Americans that Latinos are about to "take over" are overblown. The Latino presence is more and more visible on our streets and in our neighborhoods, but less visible in the political process. About half of all whites, even counting kids and immigrants, cast ballots last November, meaning it took two white residents to generate one voter. But because of a combination of lack of citizenship, a big youth population and voter apathy, only one-fifth of Hispanics went to the polls in 2004. In other words, it took five Latino residents to produce one voter.

One side effect of this is that the average Latino voter doesn't have the same profile—or the same interests and concerns—as the average Latino resident.

As with all racial and ethnic groups, registration and voting rates among Hispanics increase with age, education and income. But there is another factor unique to Hispanics; a higher share of voters were born here than in the Latino population as a whole. That means Hispanic voters and non-voters do not necessarily even speak the same language. In the general Hispanic population, the share of households where only Spanish is spoken is three times higher than among Hispanic voters.

So it should come as no surprise that when it comes to matters of policy—on immigration, trade or bilingual education—Latino voters have a different point of departure than non-voting Latinos.

Two recent issues exposed this divergence. Despite intense lobbying by the governments of several nations that have contributed millions of people to the U.S. Latino immigrant population, the Congressional Hispanic Caucus voted overwhelmingly in May to oppose the Central American Free Trade Agreement. The caucus, which is made up of Hispanic Democrats, opted for party loyalty and the perceived economic interests of the largely working-class Latino voters who put them in office over ethnic bonds to other countries.

Similarly, when Mexican President Vicente Fox made remarks widely viewed as disparaging to blacks a few weeks ago, one of the quickest condemnations came from the National Council of La Raza. The nation's largest Latino civil rights organization hewed to core principles and long-standing alliances with black groups rather than cover for the leader of a country that is by far the largest source of new immigrants.

These are signs of Hispanic politics taking root here. Hispanic political power is growing, just not as fast as one might expect from the population numbers. Moreover, as Latinos become a more prominent political presence, what we hear from them may not be what people expect.

Bush's "Real" Hispanic Numbers

By Richard Nadler
National Review, December 8, 2004

On November 3, the National Election Pool (NEP) reported that George W. Bush received 44 percent of Hispanic votes cast on November 2: a 9-percentage-point gain from his 35-percent performance in 2000. Since then, these figures have been widely challenged, and internally revised.

Ruy Teixeira of the Century Foundation estimates that 39 percent of Hispanics voted Republican. NBC, a part of the NEP pool, now calculates Bush's Latino vote at 40 percent.

Immigration critic Steve Sailer of VDARE acknowledges a 3–4 percent Bush increase, but doubts its significance. Bush's Latino gains, he writes, "confirm the general pattern that the Hispanic vote for Republicans rises and falls in the same cycles as the white vote—just consistently more Democratic."

So did Republicans make progress among Latinos in 2004? A closer examination of the NEP numbers shows that Bush's gains among Hispanics, although lower than initially estimated, were both real and significant. Specifically, the G.O.P.'s increased Latino vote share offset the potential Democrat advantage from a hefty increase in Hispanic registration and voting.

But talk of a G.O.P. "average gain" masks how that gain was distributed. In states where conservative 527 groups, such as Council for Better Government and Hispanics Together (both of which I served as a consultant), ran intensive campaigns on Spanish-language media, the president's Hispanic vote share increased sharply. In states where no such effort occurred, his Latino vote share improved hardly at all.

What is a reasonable estimate of Bush's performance among Hispanics?

The most significant internal correction by NEP pollster Edison Media Research and Mitofsky International involved Bush's Hispanic vote share in Texas. The NEP recalculated the percentage of Latinos in its Texas sample from 23 to 20 percent, and the pro-Bush Latino percentage from 59 to 49. Texas is home to 19 percent of the nation's Hispanics. This revision alone lowered Bush's national numbers 2-percentage points.

The NEP survey was by far the largest post-election poll, dwarfing those of the Los Angeles Times, the New York Times, and the Velasquez Institute. Over 13,600 respondents, including 1,100 Hispanics, completed the "long form" on which the initial Hispanic numbers were based. An additional 62,600 respondents, including 3,600 Hispanics, completed the "short form," on which the NEP based its state exit polls.

The NEP state exit polls, as published on the CNN and MSNBC websites, broke out Hispanic numbers in 20 states: That is, they gave the total number of subjects interviewed, the percent of those who were Hispanic, and the percent of Hispanics who voted for Bush and for Kerry. From this, one can calculate the number of Hispanics surveyed in each of the 20 states, and the numbers who voted for Bush and for Kerry in each.

These 20 states account for 91 percent of the nation's Hispanic population. Respondents, including 3,586 Hispanics, completed 35,891 short-form surveys. Within this 20-state set, George W. Bush won the votes of 41.28 percent of Hispanic respondents polled, compared to 57.47 for John Kerry. But the NEP sampled battleground states more heavily than non-battleground states. Rebalancing the Hispanic totals for Bush and Kerry state-by-state to reflect the Hispanic population in each relative to the total Hispanic population for the 20-state set, Bush won 38.07 percent of the Hispanic vote, compared to 59.67 for Kerry.

How significant was this gain? To political professionals, a gross three-point shift in vote share will translate into a 5 or 6 net vote shift per hundred cast. It is by the sum of such shifts, demographic group by demographic group, that elections are lost or won.

In 2000, the Voter News Service (VNS), predecessor to the NEP, reported a Gore victory among Latinos of 62-to-35 percent, or 27 votes per 100. In 2004, the NEP 20-state set, as balanced above, finds Kerry winning 59.67 percent of Hispanic votes, compared to 38.07 percent for Bush—a 21.6-vote advantage per 100.

In 2000, roughly 6 million Hispanic votes were cast. At 62-to-35 percent, this gave Gore a 1,620,000-vote victory over Bush among Latinos nationwide.

In 2004, Hispanic turnout rose by roughly 25 percent, to 7.5 million voters. Had the Democrats held their 2000 margin, their national advantage among Hispanics would have grown by 405,000, to 2,025,000. The improved Bush percentage in 2004 nullified this gain completely, holding the Democrat advantage in the Hispanic community to the same 1,620,000 as in 2000. The impact of a massive and successful Democratic voter registration drive was nullified.

Breaking It Down

But the 20-state set hides, rather than reveals, the factors that determined Republican progress (or lack thereof) among Hispanic voters. In Arizona, Nevada, Colorado, Florida, New Mexico, and Wisconsin—six battleground states, containing an NEP sample size of 1,768 Hispanic voters—conservative 527 groups ran a vigorous

12,000-spot broadcast campaign on Spanish-language media in support of the G.O.P. ticket. In the remaining 14 states, containing an NEP sample size of 1,818 Hispanic voters—no such campaign aired.

The difference in results was night-to-day. In the states where the conservative Spanish-language 527s were active, Bush carried 47.17 percent of the population-weighted Latino vote, compared to 52.25 percent for Kerry. In the 14 states where the 527s were inactive, Bush won 35.96 percent of the Hispanic vote, Kerry 61.65 percent—a result almost unchanged from Gore's 62-to-35 percent advantage of 2000.

Now, the 6 states with ads include Florida, traditionally the most Republican of the Hispanic populations. This "prior disposition" of Florida Hispanics obviously skews the 6-state set. Is there some other way to compare Bush's performance in program and non-program states?

> When Republicans have aggressively courted Hispanic votes, they have won them.

Yes. We can examine Republican vote-share changes on the margin.

Exit-poll pool member CNN lists changes in Bush's vote in 4 of the 6 "program states" on its website. Comparing the 2004 NEP state exit polls to their 2000 VNS counterparts, Bush's Hispanic share grew 5 points in Colorado, 7 in Florida, 9 in Arizona, and 12 in New Mexico. The sample size in these four states is still a healthy 1,503. Weighting these states by Hispanic population, so that the G.O.P.'s 12-point increase in New Mexico is not treated equally with, say, Florida's 7-point increase, the weighted G.O.P. increase in the 4-state sample is 7.60 percent—a shift of better than 15 votes per hundred for President Bush.

This performance was broadly consistent with the 2002 results of similar pro-G.O.P. Spanish-language broadcast campaigns, which saw top-line Republican performance in Senate and gubernatorial races increase 6.14-percentage points.

In other words, when Republicans have aggressively courted Hispanic votes, they have won them. And when we haven't, G.O.P. Latino vote-share numbers have barely budged.

Almost all conservative progress on minority media has been generated in the 527 world, by party irregulars. The official organs of the Republican Party have been missing in action, producing either weak product or no product for mass-minority audiences.

What would have happened had the Republican Party and its fellow travelers campaigned aggressively nationwide on Univision, Telemundo, and Spanish-language radio?

Extrapolating from results in the 527 program states, Kerry's projected majority of 2,025,000 votes could have been reduced by nearly half, to 1,035,000: a one million vote swing in a voting population of roughly 7.5 million.

Voting and Immigration

Steve Sailer and his friends in the anti-immigration lobby regularly criticize efforts to woo Hispanic voters two ways. First, they contend that the Hispanic vote "tracks" the white vote anyhow, making such efforts superfluous. Second, they contend such efforts constitute a sell-out to advocates of open borders and mass immigration.

The Hispanic vote does not track the white vote. Above, we've seen that the Hispanic vote "tracks" what's happening on the ground in particular places, not some macro-trend. But even in its generalized (i.e., irrelevant) form, this assertion is untrue. Look at the trends in white and Hispanic voting for Republican presidential candidates over the last 28 years in the New York Times exit polls:

1976–1980: White vote +4   Hispanic vote +9

1980–1984: White vote +8   Hispanic vote +4

1984–1988: White vote -5   Hispanic vote -7

1988–1992: White vote -19   Hispanic vote -9

1992–1996: White vote +6   Hispanic vote -4

1996–2000: White vote +8   Hispanic vote +10

Over the entire period, the average variation between changes in white and Hispanic voting was 5.5 points per election. To an election strategist, these figures signal wild variation. Any professional looking at those numbers would seek independent variables to explain them. And the first thing he'd examine is differences in the communications that the two groups are receiving.

The second assertion—that Spanish-language campaigns are a sell-out to advocates of open borders—is a non sequitur. The ads of Republican 527s could have been so designed. In fact, they were not. In 2002, the Council for Better Government campaigns featured 15 scripts, not one of which dealt with immigration. In 2004, two scripts of 32 aired by the council and Hispanics Together broached the subject, defending the president's policy. But the overwhelming preponderance of the spots dealt with traditional conservative issues. Scripts advocated traditional marriage, tax breaks for families and small business, school choice, military preparedness, the right to life, personal savings accounts, and faith-based social-service delivery. Given the steeply rising percentage of Hispanics who supported George Bush in the "527 program" states, one may conclude that conservative issues gained considerable traction among them.

The complaint conservatives lodge against open immigration is that it fosters the balkanization of our nation, creating enclaves of "hyphenated Americans" ideologically isolated from our values, but parasitically attached to our pocketbooks. But whether our borders are thrown wide open or slammed tightly shut, it is hard to see how conservatives, by ignoring 7.5 million Hispanic voters, will make them less balkanized, or less liberal.

G.O.P. Risking Hispanic Votes on Immigration

By David D. Kirkpatrick
The New York Times, March 30, 2006

The battle among Republicans over immigration policy and border security is threatening to undercut a decade-long effort by President Bush and his party to court Hispanic voters, just as both parties are gearing up for the 2006 elections.

"I believe the Republican Party has hurt itself already," said the Rev. Luis Cortes, a Philadelphia pastor close to President Bush and the leader of a national organization of Hispanic Protestant clergy members, saying he delivered that message to the president last week in a meeting at the White House.

To underscore the contested allegiance of Hispanic voters, Mr. Cortes said, he also took a delegation of Hispanic ministers to meet with the leaders of both parties last week, including what he called a productive discussion with Howard Dean, the Democratic chairman.

The immigration and security debate, which has sparked huge demonstrations in recent days by Hispanic residents of cities around the country, comes at a crucial moment for both parties.

Over the last three national elections, persistent appeals by Mr. Bush and other Republican leaders have helped double their party's share of the Hispanic vote, to more than 40 percent in 2004 from about 20 percent in 1996. As a result, Democrats can no longer rely on the country's 42 million Hispanic residents as a natural part of their base.

In a lunch meeting of Senate Republicans this week, Senator Mel Martinez of Florida, the only Hispanic Republican in the Senate, gave his colleagues a stern warning. "This is the first issue that, in my mind, has absolutely galvanized the Latino community in America like no other," Mr. Martinez said he told them.

The anger among Hispanics has continued even as the Senate Judiciary Committee proposed a bill this week that would allow illegal immigrants a way to become citizens. The backlash was aggravated, Mr. Martinez said in an interview, by a Republican plan to crack down on illegal immigrants that the House approved last year.

The outcome remains to be seen. Speaker J. Dennis Hastert said on Wednesday that he recognized the need for a guest-worker program, opening the door to a possible compromise on fiercely debated immigration legislation.

Democrats see an opportunity to "show Hispanics who their real friends are," as Senator Charles E. Schumer of New York, chairman of the Democratic Senatorial Campaign Committee, put it.

But the issue is a delicate matter for Democrats as well. Polls show large majorities of the public both support tighter borders as a matter of national security, and oppose amnesty for illegal immigrants. Many working-class Democrats resent what they see as a continuing influx of cheap labor.

The stakes are enormous because Hispanics now account for one of every eight United States residents, and for about half the recent growth in the country's population. Although Hispanics cast just 6 percent of the votes in the 2004 elections, birth rates promise an imminent explosion in the number of eligible voters.

Polls show large majorities of the public both support tighter borders as a matter of national security, and oppose amnesty for illegal immigrants.

"There is a big demographic wave of Hispanic kids who are native born who will be turning 18 in even greater numbers over the next three, four and five election cycles," Roberto Suro, director of the nonpartisan Pew Hispanic Center, said.

Nowhere is the immigration debate more heated than Arizona, where about 28 percent of the population is Hispanic and where Senator Jon Kyl, a Republican sponsor of an immigration bill, faces what could be a difficult race for re-election. Both Mr. Kyl and his Democratic challenger, Jim Pederson, have hired Hispanics or Hispanic-dominated firms to manage their campaigns.

A mostly Hispanic crowd of about 20,000 gathered outside Mr. Kyl's office last weekend to protest criminal penalties against illegal immigrants that were in the House Republican bill, even though Mr. Kyl's proposal does not include the measure.

Mario E. Diaz, the campaign manager for Mr. Pederson, faulted Mr. Kyl's proposal, which would require illegal immigrants or future temporary workers to return to their countries before becoming eligible for legal status in the United States.

"Speaking the language that Kyl does, which is round them up and deport them, is offensive and disgusting to the Latino community," Mr. Diaz said.

Mr. Kyl, for his part, accused Democrats of race-baiting by painting all Republicans as anti-Hispanic, a practice he said most Hispanics resent. But the senator also acknowledged some fears that the immigration debate could repel Hispanic voters. He added, "I would hope that some of our colleagues who don't have much of a Hispanic population in their states would at least defer to those of us who do."

Pollsters from each party say Hispanics, like other groups, typically rank immigration lower in importance than other issues, especially education. But they respond strongly when they believe the rhetoric surrounding the debate demonizes immigrants or Hispanics, as they did when Gov. Pete Wilson of California, a Republican, backed a 1994 initiative to exclude illegal immigrants from public schools and services.

Many analysts say the backlash from Hispanics wrecked the California Republican Party for a decade.

As governor of Texas, Mr. Bush opposed such measures, and pushed Republicans to woo Hispanics.

Last week, Sergio Bendixen, a pollster for the Democratic Senatorial Campaign Committee, released a rare multilingual poll in which 76 percent of legal Latin American immigrants said they believed anti-immigrant sentiment was on the rise. A majority of immigrants said they believed the immigration debate was unfair and misinformed.

But Ken Mehlman, chairman of the Republican National Committee, dismissed such concerns. Mr. Mehlman said the party's image was defined by President Bush, who supports a temporary-worker program and has repeatedly urged Republicans to avoid inflammatory rhetoric.

"In an emotional debate like this," Mr. Mehlman said, "people need to lower their energy and remember that ultimately the goal is something that is consistent with being a nation of laws and a nation of immigrants."

Danny Diaz, a spokesman for the Republican Party, said it had pushed ahead on recruitment of Hispanic candidates and voters. He noted that Mr. Mehlman had appeared frequently at events with Hispanic groups, hitting classic Republican themes about lower taxes and traditional values. A particular focus has been Hispanic churchgoers and pastors like Mr. Cortes, who receives money from Mr. Bush's religion-based social services initiative.

Democrats say that Mr. Bush's success with Hispanics has not gone unnoticed. Democratic leaders in Congress have expanded their Spanish-language communications, and after 2004 the Democratic Party vowed to stop relying on payments to Hispanic groups and organizations to help turn out Hispanic voters.

"How can you spend your money on get-out-the-vote when you are beginning to lose your market share?" Mr. Bendixen said. "But Democrats had no experience in campaigning for the hearts and minds of Hispanic voters. They treated them like black voters who they just needed to get out to the polls."

Still, both sides say it is the tenor and ultimate outcome of the immigration debate that may give the Democrats their best opportunity to attract Hispanic voters.

Senator Martinez, a Cuban immigrant who delivered part of a Senate speech in Spanish a few months ago, alluded to the nervousness among Hispanics when he was asked whether he would do the same again in the debate on immigration. "I am about to be sent back as it is," he said, joking. "I better be careful."

IV. Cultural and Economic Influence

Editor's Introduction

One of the major trends in American culture in recent years has been the growing influence of a distinct Hispanic-American identity. Indeed, as Jordan Levin remarks in "A Nueve Generation," the first article in this chapter, "an exploding generation of bilingual, bicultural Hispanics . . . are rapidly emerging as a force that will affect music, television, movies, fashion, advertising, slang, and just about everything else in American pop culture." This trend, highlighted by such performers as Jennifer Lopez, Eva Longoria, Jimmy Smits, and George Lopez, among others, has developed considerable momentum of late and is beginning to leave an indelible mark on the American mosaic. As this cultural emergence has taken place, Latino economic influence has likewise expanded.

Levin's piece explores these trends from a broad perspective, emphasizing the Latino impact on various industries and artistic forms. The next entry, "Grading Hispanic Gains on TV? Start with ABC," by Eric Deggans, takes a much more specific approach, focusing on the growing Hispanic presence on television and the strategies used by television executives to attract the highly prized Latino demographic.

Another medium with a blossoming Hispanic-American influence is the Internet. As Alan Sipress notes in the subsequent piece, "Hispanics' Web Identity Grows as Ads Target Diverse Audience," the influence goes both ways, with the World Wide Web providing a symbiotic and nuanced forum for American Latinos that is used by advertisers and executives to attract the demographic, while also providing Hispanics with the means to access American culture and to maintain connections with their home countries.

Increasingly, those looking to attract Hispanic consumers are addressing their appeals in English, thus offering a vivid counterpoint to some who argue that the language barrier between Latinos and native English speakers is becoming problematic. Leon Lazaroff discusses this trend in the following entry, "English Enters into Media for Latinos." This pattern is further examined in the next piece, "Latino Marketing Goes Mainstream," by Samar Farah, which examines a particular Super Bowl ad. Given the Super Bowl's high ratings—and exalted status in American life—advertisers do their best to make commercials that air during the game as groundbreaking and engaging as possible. Consequently, when Toyota ran an ad featuring a man with an Hispanic accent during the Super Bowl in February 2006, the advertising and marketing industry took notice. As Farah observes, the ad was a watershed moment, heralding not only the arrival of Hispanic Americans as an essential consumer market, but also suggesting that the most effective way to appeal to them was in English.

Among the reasons Hispanic Americans are so prized by advertisers and media companies is that they tend to be younger and thus more upwardly mobile than other groups. Ben White, in "Pursuing Hispanic Wealth," discusses how big business and the financial sector are seeking to attract these up-and-coming Hispanic consumers and the capital they are likely to generate.

A Nueve Generation

By Jordan Levin
The Miami Herald, September 3, 2006

In the 1960s and '70s, it was baby boomers with rock and disco, sexual liberation and political activism. In the '80s and '90s, it was African Americans and hip-hop that transformed the way we sang, danced, talked and dressed.

And now, at the start of the 21st century, it's a new generation of Hispanics who are poised to become the next major cultural drivers.

While the political spotlight has been on Hispanic immigrants, social scholars and purveyors of media and entertainment are already focusing on their children, an exploding generation of bilingual, bicultural Hispanics who are rapidly emerging as a force that will affect music, television, movies, fashion, advertising, slang and just about everything else in American pop culture.

Because they grew up in the United States fluent in two languages and two cultures, young American-born Hispanics—who often call themselves Latinos, rather than Hispanics—form a kind of bridge. Not only are they Latinizing the American mainstream, they are Americanizing what it means to be Hispanic in the United States.

"What Americans and even Latinos need to understand is that there's a movement, and that movement is *todos los Latinos* that practice the traditions of where they're from, but at the same time they have that American influence," says Isis Velasquez, a 21-year-old student at the University of Florida.

Demographic Shift

The movement is driven by numbers.

Second-generation Hispanics are the fastest-growing portion of this country's largest minority, and by 2020 they will outnumber their immigrant parents.

Their numbers are increasing more quickly than those of their white or black counterparts in the younger age groups that shape culture.

One in five people in the United States younger than 18—the age group over which marketers salivate—are Hispanic.

"Our influence is going to be felt," says film director Franc Reyes, whose movie *Illegal Tender*, a thriller with a Hispanic cast, will be released by Universal this fall.

"You can't put that many people under a rug and say they don't exist before some of us start screaming—artistically or whatever way."

But it's not just about numbers.

Whether it's the beat of reggaeton booming across America or the dark-haired, dark-eyed Mexican-American actress Eva Longoria becoming the hottest thing on *Desperate Housewives*, Hispanics are happening.

"This is just the beginning of what's going to be a profound impact over the lifetime of a generation," says Christy Haubegger, who represents stars such as Salma Hayek, Antonio Banderas, Shakira and Marc Anthony for the powerful Hollywood talent agency CAA.

A decade ago, Haubegger launched *Latina*, the women's magazine that pioneered speaking to this bicultural audience with a Spanglishized "Hey, chica!" style and features on everything from fashion for curvier bodies to health issues affecting Hispanics.

"This is just the beginning of what's going to be a profound impact over the lifetime of a generation."—Christy Haubegger, Hollywood talent agent

---

Influencing America

Haubegger says that as American companies reach out to this new market, the new generation of Hispanics is influencing America in return.

"This bicultural, fast-growing population certainly is a remarkably attractive and fast-growing market in itself," Haubegger says.

But that's not all. "It's a group that is incredibly geographically concentrated in the cultural sections of America," Haubegger says. "As a result, we are able to exert a disproportionate influence on entertainment, on culture, on music, on fashion, on all these things that define America."

The signs of that redefinition are everywhere:

In September, ABC will add Hayek's production of *Ugly Betty*, based on the popular Spanish-language telenovela, to a lineup that already includes the successful sitcom *George Lopez*.

Shakira's Spanglish, reggaeton-inflected song *Hips Don't Lie* (with Haitian rapper Wyclef Jean) topped the pop charts for several weeks this spring.

Puerto Rican reggaeton star Daddy Yankee has joined hip-hop acts 50 Cent and Jay-Z in marketing his own Reebok sneaker.

One of this summer's top-selling pop tours was Mexican teen group RBD, which will soon launch an English-language album.

MTV en Español, the U.S. Spanish-language branch of the trendsetting music/lifestyle network, is changing its name to MTV Tr3s and revamping its programming to appeal to kids as hot for 50

Cent as they are for Juanes, the multimillion-selling Colombian rocker who fills venues like Madison Square Garden and Broward County's BankAtlantic Center.

Telemundo's cable channel mun2 is adding programs like *The Chicas Project*, about a pair of hip Latinas juggling "beauty tips, boy trouble, and lunch at *abuela's*" for young audiences hungry for shows that reflect their culture-straddling lives.

A 2003 study by Roberto Suro, director of the Washington-based Pew Hispanic Center, showed the numbers behind the trend. Suro's study established not only that the second generation is becoming the most important segment of Hispanics, but that they are also the ones to watch in the general population.

Because Hispanics have more children than other ethnic groups—3.51 births per woman, compared with 1.84 for non-Hispanic whites and 2.53 for blacks—and because non-Hispanic whites are predicted to fall below 50 percent of the population by 2050, Latinos are poised to become even more significant.

Advertisers and Hollywood producers are starting to cater to Hispanics

---

"Getting Latinized"

According to Suro, U.S. Hispanics make up 19 percent of people 20 to 34 years old, the crucial years when people move into adulthood and establish careers. By 2020, Latinos will make up almost one-fourth of children 5 to 19, a study by the California consulting firm Cheskin predicted.

"In terms of that market that really defines popular culture, it's getting Latinized much faster than the rest of the population," Suro says.

That is of intense interest to U.S. companies.

"All of them are slowly waking up to the fact that moving forward, this is the fastest-growing sector of the U.S. economy," says Marcel Suarez-Orozco, co-director of the Harvard Immigration Project and coauthor of the book *Children of Immigration*.

"This is where the action will be in terms of new investment, new growth. So even though the attention is on immigrants, even if we seal the border tomorrow, the real growth will be in the second generation."

Advertisers and Hollywood producers are starting to cater to Hispanics—a change that decades of protests by Hispanic advocacy groups about a lack of representation in the media weren't able to create.

"They're seeing demographically they've got to start serving the Hispanic population or they'll be left behind," says Gabriel Reyes of Reyes Entertainment, a Hollywood marketing and public-relations company.

"Network TV audiences have been shrinking for years, so if this is a whole crop of new audiences and it's growing, that's very attractive."

ABC has such high expectations for Hayek's *Ugly Betty* that it has scheduled the program for Thursday nights against popular shows such as *Survivor, My Name Is Earl* and *The Office.* Hayek believes Hispanic viewers are eager to see a popular character and story from their culture on English-language TV.

"Although there are some things out there for the Latin market to see, I think the potential that's out there has not been tapped into," she says.

Despite predictions for the future and the emergence of Hispanic faces and voices in mainstream culture, many young Hispanics still believe they are underrepresented—and when they are, it's often in negative stereotypes.

Image in the Media

"There's so many of us and we're so different, but we're just not depicted in the media," says Lara Coppola, 24, who was born in Venezuela to Italian Jewish par+-ents and came to Miami at 11.

"With the mainstream Latin stuff like reggaeton, it becomes like self-stereotyping, almost like this Latin minstrelsy," says her friend Arielle Castillo, 22. "It's like all Latinos are a certain way."

But things are changing. There are more Hispanics on network television—ABC's fall lineup features several, including Colombian actress Sofia Vergara on the comedy series *Knights of Prosperity,* and Jay Hernandez in a drama called *Six Degrees.* Carlos Mencia's *Mind of Mencia* is the second most popular show on Comedy Central.

Jennifer Lopez is producing the movie *Border Town,* about the murder of women in the Mexican city of Juárez, starring Lopez and Antonio Banderas and directed by Gregory Nava (who oversaw Lopez in *Selena*).

Lopez is also co-starring with her husband, singer-actor Marc Anthony, in *El Cantante,* about pioneering salsa singer Hector Lavoe.

Corporations are shifting from marketing exclusively to Hispanics in Spanish and in traditional Hispanic media to reaching them in English in mainstream outlets.

Toyota ran an ad for its new 2007 Camry Hybrid on the Super Bowl telecast that used the way a Hispanic father and son switch languages as a metaphor for the car.

"*Mira aquí* [look here]," the father says to his son, as he explains how the car switches between gasoline and electric power and how it's "better for our future."

"Like you with English and Spanish," the boy chirps.

"A Huge Trend"

Kim McCullough, corporate manager of marketing communications for Toyota, says the bicultural, bilingual message is important. "We recognize this is a huge trend that we need to be ahead of and not just responding to," she says.

"Companies are definitely realizing that some Hispanics are more comfortable if they are spoken to in English," says Carlos Martinez, general manager of the Hispanic advertising agency Conill LA, which created the Toyota spot.

"So, you will definitely see more of this bilingual advertising."

The message goes both ways. Reebok signed reggaeton star Daddy Yankee to put his name on a line of sneakers primarily because the company thought he would appeal to Hispanics, but also because it thought he would connect with mainstream customers.

But figuring out how to reach this generation can be difficult, in part because these children of immigrants are still figuring out the unique mix of language, culture and identity that goes with being Hispanic—or Latino—in this country.

"The word *Latino* doesn't exist outside of the United States," says José Tillan, senior vice president of music programming and talent strategy for MTV Latin America and MTV Tr3s.

"It's like a new world. The definition of the word *Latino* is up for grabs."

If to be American is to invent yourself, young Hispanics are as American as it gets, stitching together a patchwork of references and identities in two languages with surprising optimism and confidence.

"I think Latinas in general have a better advantage," says 13-year-old Miami student Shawn Nelson, whose background is Cuban, Puerto Rican, Jamaican and Trinidadian.

"I'm never just black or I'm never just Cuban. I can be around anybody and still be who I want to be."

Grading Hispanic Gains on TV? Start with ABC

BY ERIC DEGGANS
ST. PETERSBURG TIMES, DECEMBER 8, 2005

A few months ago, I asked ABC entertainment president Stephen McPherson a question: Given the huge increase in Hispanic actors on its fall lineup, was the network deliberately trying to make its casts more diverse?

"We're not out there trying to actively hire more Hispanics," said McPherson, still high on his reputation as the guy who saved the alphabet network with hits such as Lost and Desperate Housewives. "We try to be colorblind and get the best actor or actress for any role."

I figured it was the typical head fake by a network executive: Pretend you're not doing something you clearly are doing, with full knowledge the media will give you credit for something you fear may upset viewers if you actually admitted it.

But McPherson was more explicit with the New York Post, telling the newspaper in a Nov. 21 story, "I think it's been part of our initiative for a couple of years and it's something that's important to me. . . . I look at it as a business decision. There's a gigantic Hispanic audience out there."

To this, I say just one thing: It's about time.

For many years, Hispanics have been the most under-represented minority on television, with a 2000 study revealing that the country's largest ethnic minority—about 14 percent of the population—filled about 2 percent of roles in prime time.

But years of steady increases in population (35.3-million in 2000 to 41.3-million in 2004, according to the U.S. Census) and buying power ($404-billion in 2000 to $686-billion in 2004, according to the Selig Center for Economic Growth) have brought a new reality in network TV, particularly at ABC.

The National Latino Media Council recognized the network TV industry's success last week in its annual report card for 2005, handing high marks to most networks for strides in casting, program development and hiring among writers and producers.

It was a striking change from fall 1999, when the council joined other groups to complain that no people of color were featured in the casts of new series at the top four TV networks.

"The diversity programs that were begun four and five years ago are now bearing fruit," NLMC president Alex Nogales said in a statement. "What (Latinos) contribute to our nation has to be more clear, so this perception counters the view of the bigots among us."

> It's not just ABC that has finally awakened to the reality of diversity.

On ABC, there's Freddie Prinze Jr.'s hit sitcom Freddie, Lost's latest take-charge leader Michelle Rodriguez, Eddie Cibrian's grown-up Cuban immigrant on Invasion and new Grey's Anatomy cast member Sara Ramirez; ABC has moved aggressively this season to ensure nearly every show has a Hispanic actor in its core cast.

The network's news department followed suit this week, naming Elizabeth Vargas co-anchor of World News Tonight, making her the first Hispanic to reach the top job in network TV evening news.

It's what you might expect from the network that also was the first to feature subtitles or secondary audio programs offering Spanish translations for all its prime-time shows. They also offered the first regular series character who only speaks Spanish with English subtitles: the character of Prinze's grandmother, who appears on a show featuring four Hispanic actors.

And it's not just ABC that has finally awakened to the reality of diversity. Look to NBC and see Benjamin Bratt on NBC's E-Ring (okay, he does play a guy named J .T. Tisnewski—with no explanation of the guy's heritage), John Leguizamo in a high-profile turn on ER, Miguel Sandoval as a down-to-earth district attorney on Medium and Jimmy Smits running for president on The West Wing.

Behind the scenes, Greg Garcia (whose great-grandfather was Mexican entertainer Cantinflas) is producing NBC's only comedy hit, My Name is Earl, while Jennifer Lopez's Nuyorican Films production company is developing the night-time soap opera South Beach for UPN.

Considering that last season there were only three new TV series prominently featuring Hispanics—Lost, Housewives and UPN's ill-fated Jonny Zero—this year's surge in new characters feels like a virtual avalanche.

"I'm the youngest executive producer ABC has ever had, and I'm the only Puerto Rican," Prinze said. "You think about the number of Hispanics who have led their own (successful sitcoms), and you've got something like four in the history of this business."

Five years ago, Freddie executive producer Bruce Helford quizzed ABC executives on whether they were serious about airing a sitcom pilot featuring an up-and-coming Mexican comic named George Lopez. Now that Lopez's self-titled sitcom is a hit, Helford sees the network taking the next logical step.

"It's a huge financial risk—each pilot costs a couple million—and until George's show, there had been no successful (Hispanic cast) shows," Helford said. "They believed in George's show, believed in more Hispanic representation, and now, for everybody, it makes sense to take more risk."

Indeed, statistics show Hispanics watch an average four more hours of prime-time TV each week and have a median age nearly 10 years younger than the general population. Why wouldn't a smart network go after a wealthier, younger segment of the population that the TV industry has traditionally ignored?

"We know that the Hispanic audience has a very powerful voice," said CBS entertainment president Nina Tassler, whose self-described "Russia-rican" heritage (Russian father, Puerto Rican mother) likely makes her the most powerful Hispanic woman in network TV. "This year, we really tried to increase the numbers of Hispanics in our existing shows and our new shows. It is increasingly important to our advertisers."

A look at the top-rated English-language TV shows in Hispanic households shows the strategy may be paying off.

Just a couple of years ago, that roster was topped by shows such as American Idol and Fear Factor; during the week of Nov. 14, it included four ABC series featuring Hispanics in prominent roles: Desperate Housewives, Lost, George Lopez and Freddie.

Already, viewers have reaped benefits with more complex and varied characters, from Eva Longoria and Ricardo Chavira's bickering couple on Desperate Housewives to Cibrian's grown-up Cuban orphan on Invasion. Such characters are a welcome relief from the parade of gang-bangers, gardeners and maids Hispanic actors were often forced to play.

Still, such close counting sometimes feels awkward, even to Hispanic actors who would like to see more diversity in the industry.

Actor Kiele Sanchez, whose blond hair and blue eyes belie her Puerto Rican and French heritage, has never played a Latina on screen, and is currently cast as an Italian woman on the WB drama series Related. She often jokes about such issues with co-star Jennifer Esposito, a New York–born Italian who is often cast as a Hispanic woman—most recently in the hit film, Crash.

"I've never played a Hispanic, because people don't believe that I am," Sanchez said. "The image people still have in the industry is that Latinas have to have dark hair, dark eyes and dark skin. It's like, have you turned on Telemundo lately?"

Meanwhile, other ethnic minorities, particularly Asian-Americans, have criticized stagnant hiring levels for their groups. And former NYPD Blue star Esai Morales remains wary the current hiring boom will fade.

"We live in a world that is so media saturated, if the media doesn't show it, the public doesn't know it," Morales said in an interview earlier this year. "And if people of ethnicity are not allowed to express their own reality, then they are being suppressed."

Hispanics' Web Identity Grows as Ads Target Diverse Audience

By Alan Sipress
The Washington Post, October 7, 2006

Alberto Otero moved from Puerto Rico to Washington as a boy and grew up listening to the old salsa records his parents played to remind them of home.

Five years ago, he began getting his fix of salsa from an Hispanic music Web site called Batanga.com. When a melody grew repetitive, he surfed across the other genres of Latin music featured on the site and soon discovered a taste for the loping, rolling songs from Colombia known as cumbia, the Cuban dance rhythms of cubanisimo and urban American Hispanic music called reggaeton. The offerings of the Internet, he said, helped reshape his sense of what it meant to be Hispanic.

"I'm thinking of myself as an American Latino," said Otero, 30, an education counselor. "This has broadened me."

Today, a contest over Hispanic identity is being waged on the terrain of the Internet. The proliferation of Web sites such as Batanga, which appeal to Latinos regardless of where they come from, is pulling in one direction, encouraging the emergence of a wider Hispanic identity that transcends the borders that long fragmented the group. But a countervailing trend, which taps into the endless specialization available on the Web, is pushing the opposite way, toward a narrower identity rooted in homeland and even in hometown.

"The Internet allows you to develop a greater identity, but you can still find out the weather in your parents' hometown," said Rebeca Logan, a former news producer at AOL Latino.

Motivated by commercial considerations, Web sites such as AOL Latino, Univision.com, Yahoo-Telemundo and Batanga are trying to capture as large an Hispanic audience as possible in a bid for advertisers. The interest in that market is soaring, with advertisers more than tripling the amount they spend online targeting U.S. Hispanics in just the last year, said Lee Vann, co-founder of the Captura Group, an online Hispanic marketing firm.

These Web sites, often with an emphasis on culture, entertainment and immigration issues, are accelerating an established trend among U.S.–born Hispanics toward a pan-Latino identity, researchers and marketers said.

"The Internet is facilitating a lot of interaction and learning from each other," said Felipe Korzenny, an expert in Hispanic marketing at Florida State University. "Groups are becoming more flexible and more appreciative across countries."

But the Web has also made it possible for Hispanics in the United States to remain plugged into the news and culture of their ancestral lands by reading the more than 700 Latin American newspapers now online. Other niche sites, along with e-mail, Internet telephone services, instant messaging and social-networking sites such as MySpace.com and Quepasa.com, are allowing Hispanics to stay in daily contact with their families—and their local identities—as never before.

"You don't have to leave behind where you come from," said Donald A. DePalma, president of Common Sense Advisory Inc., a market research firm. "You can assimilate . . . but when you go home, you can get your online equivalent of comfort food."

Though many ethnic groups claim their identity runs in their blood, technology has long played a decisive role in how people see themselves. It was the advent of the printing press in the 15th century that shaped the European ethnic groups of today by introducing the mass publication of books in a limited number of standard European languages. Speakers of French, English and other European vernaculars increasingly began to identify with others who spoke the same language, planting the seeds for modern nations.

> Few technological developments have promised to reshape ethnic identities as dramatically as the Web.

Since then, few technological developments have promised to reshape ethnic identities as dramatically as the Web.

Spanish-language television started forging a pan-Latino identity among American Hispanics more than two decades ago. Broadcasters, especially the longtime king of the Spanish-language airwaves, Univision, began introducing a standardized Spanish for news programs that would appeal to Latinos regardless of their home countries, Korzenny said. More recently, its main network competitor, Telemundo introduced a policy that actors in the fabulously popular telenovelas be coached to speak in a neutral, flat Spanish without any of the idiosyncrasies associated with one country or another.

The Internet is now accelerating this trend, he said.

Gustavo Paredes, 51, was raised in Adams Morgan, the son of immigrants from Colombia and the Dominican Republic, and had spent much of his life listening to the melodious, often breezy music of those two countries like salsa and merengue. But after he began experimenting with different channels on Batanga, he found he was unexpectedly drawn to songs from Mexico, which their unique rhythms and lyrics that often speak of pain, pride and loneliness.

This "cross-pollination," Paredes said, "broadens the identity of Latinos."

Offering two dozen online Latin music channels from countries running the length of Latin America plus Spain, Batanga.com has nearly doubled its audience in the last year, to 1.4 million unique visitors a month, according to comScore Media Metrix, which measures Internet audiences for analysts and marketers. Batanga has recently extended its reach, merging with PlanetaTV.com to offer thousands of Latin music videos.

"Music is a huge cultural glue that is beginning to transcend your country and the country of your parents," Batanga chief executive Rafael Urbina-Quintero said. "We find a new kind of Hispanic culture is being born here in the United States."

But while many Hispanics are reaching out, others, like Francisco Maravilla, are reaching back. Maravilla, 42, moved to Gaithersburg six years ago from the small town of San Juan Nonualco, El Salvador, eventually got his green card and has never returned. But every day, he said, he logs on to the computer, calls up the sites of two main Salvadoran newspapers, La Prensa Grafica and El Diario de Hoy, and navigates to the pages with news from his home province, where the rest of his family still lives.

"How can I forget my country? I can never do that," said Maravilla, who is employed as a school maintenance worker.

He also checks his hometown's Web site about twice a month to keep up with local happenings and view photographs of local festivals. "No doubt about it," he said, "the Web site keeps me feeling proud of my country and where I lived."

The combination of ample band width and niche marketing means the Internet can offer myriad cultural touchstones from the old country, ranging from ingredients for specialty dishes to traditional music for the holidays.

Yet online newspapers—there are more than 100 from Mexico alone—have emerged as the main way to stay connected. A study by the Pew Hispanic Center two years ago found that the Internet was one of the main ways that Hispanics in the United States kept informed about events in their country of origin.

Paula Avila, 24, came to Arlington nearly two years ago from Colombia and quickly turned to the Internet for news. Raised in the remote town of Yopel, she said she waits anxiously for the local monthly newspaper to update its site. More often, Avila turns to the Web site of the national newspaper, El Tiempo, published in the capital, Bogota, where she studied law.

Soon after her arrival, she also began to miss sitting around the television with her family to watch Colombian soap operas. Telenovelas on Spanish-language television in the United States failed to satisfy, lacking the Colombian "cultural signature." So Avila said she started visiting the Web site of a Colombian television station and watching the daily soap opera previews posted there.

But it remains the newspaper Web sites that are the main reminder of who she is, Avila said.

"I want to keep feeling proud of my country and my city and my people," she said. "Following the news makes it easier to feel I still come from Colombia and to feel my identity."

English Enters into Media for Latinos

By Leon Lazaroff
Chicago Tribune, August 5, 2005

Eager to reach younger and more affluent U.S. Hispanics, advertisers, publishers and cable television networks are discovering it is best to speak to them in their own language—English.

Spanish may be the dominant language of Latinos, the fastest-growing ethnic group in the country. However, for bilingual, better-educated young Hispanics, English increasingly is the media language of choice.

In response, a new crop of English-language television networks, radio stations and magazines have emerged to offer fresh choices to "acculturated" Latinos, those who maintain their Latin roots but identify closely with the American mainstream.

"Marketers have long been frustrated that there aren't enough media channels to reach bilingual, bicultural Hispanics," said Erika Prosper, strategy director at Garcia 360Communications, an agency based in San Antonio. "It makes sense that when you look at your total Hispanic marketing plan that not 100 percent goes into Spanish-language media."

The choices for English-leaning Latinos are multiplying. On television there's SiTV, the English-language cable network launched last year that targets hip, young Hispanics but is designed to appeal to anyone 18 to 34 years old. Likewise, the Spanish-language network Telemundo's sister channel Mun2—a play on the Spanish word mundos, or worlds—uses English to reach young and more acculturated Hispanics.

On radio, roughly a dozen stations, owned by large media groups such as Clear Channel Communications and Spanish Broadcasting Systems, have converted in the past year to an "Hurban" format, in which disc jockeys speak in English but play music in Spanish and English.

Among magazines, the move to capture the acculturated Latino has been even more pronounced. Marcos Baer, publisher of the Hispanic media industry newsletter Portada, or front page, said more than a dozen English-language magazines catering to Hispanics have launched in the past year.

More Voices in the Mix

They include Loft, a lifestyle and entertainment monthly published in Miami that targets "sophisticated and affluent" Hispanic men; iCaramba U., a New York–based bimonthly aimed at Latino high school and college students; Bello, or Beauty, an upscale lifestyle quarterly published in Santa Ana, Calif.; and Hombre, meaning man, a men's title along the lines of Esquire.

Those new publications join more-established English-language publications such as Urban Latino, Hispanic Business, Latina and Catalina.

"The biggest hole we've had in our market are media that speak to us intelligently," said Jaime Gamboa, publisher of *Tu Ciudad*, or Your City, a Los Angeles magazine owned by Emmis Communications. Emmis, which introduced Tu Ciudad in May, plans to roll out similar editions in other U.S. cities, including Chicago.

"We're looking for voices that speak to us about what's going on in our lives, and speak to us in the language we use every day, which is English," said Gamboa, referring to acculturated Latinos.

"We're looking for voices that speak to us about
what's going on in our lives, and speak to us in the
language we use every day, which is English."—
Jaime Gamboa, publisher of TU CIUDAD magazine

To be sure, the vast majority of advertising aimed at Hispanics is done in Spanish.

Of the about $3.4 billion to be spent on Hispanic advertising in 2005, the percentage of English-language spending will not rise above the low single digits, said Alex Lopez Negrete, president of Houston-based Lopez Negrete Communications and chairman of the Association of Hispanic Advertising Agencies.

English-language outlets may not generate the kind of revenues produced by their Spanish-language counterparts, but their very existence reflects important changes in the composition of U.S. Hispanics, said Roberto Suro, director of the Pew Hispanic Center, a research institute in Washington.

As the population of American-born Hispanics has increased, so has bilingualism, Suro said. According to Pew's 2002 National Survey of Latinos, 46 percent of second-generation and 78 percent of third-generation adult Hispanics speak mostly English. Drawing a connection between income and language, HispanTelligence, the research arm of Hispanic Business Inc., reported in December that English-dominant Hispanics account for 59 percent of Hispanics' spending power.

As of 2004, Hispanics represent the country's largest minority group, totaling roughly 41 million people, or 14 percent of the population, the Census Bureau reported. For advertisers, one of the most significant census findings was that more than 31 percent of Hispanics are 18 to 34 years old, a group prized for its brand-conscious, free-spending ways.

But the census also revealed that American-born Hispanics, not immigrants, accounted for 60 percent of the growth in the Latino population since 2000. Rather than shedding their roots and completely assimilating into U.S. culture, these Hispanics, Suro said, "acculturate—they identify themselves as Hispanic and American."

The question for media companies and advertisers is how best to reach this evolving population.

"Spreading Their Bets"

"The unknown here is the extent to which someone retains an ethnic identity that influences their choices of entertainment," Suro said. "It's a large enough population that marketers are spreading their bets."

General Motors has become one of the most active advertisers among English-language Hispanic media. Felipe Herrera, GM's director of Hispanic marketing, explains that over the past four or five years corporate advertisers began to tailor campaigns to better connect with certain demographic groups.

"Second- and third-generation Hispanics' use of language might be different than more recent immigrants, so we've had to accompany that shift by expanding our outreach," he said.

Until recently, television advertisers aiming at acculturated Hispanics could choose only from networks in the English-language general market or broad-based Spanish-language outlets, principally Univision Communications or its chief rival, NBC's Telemundo.

But reaching Hispanics who prefer English by advertising on a popular show such as Fox's "American Idol" can have its downside, said Lisa Contreras-Torres, director of multicultural services at Carat USA, a media services group. Hispanics want to see something in a commercial that speaks specifically to them, she said.

"What appeals to someone in the general market may not appeal to someone who is English-speaking of Latin descent," Contreras-Torres said. "At the same time, it's not as simple as Univision equals your entire Hispanic campaign."

Though the number of English-language media aimed at Hispanics has grown, Tom McGarrity, head of network sales at Univision, doubts they will make much of an impact on how corporate advertisers spend their money.

Spanish-language television now receives more than 64 percent of all advertising aimed at Hispanics. Univision gets 78 percent of that television spending, while Telemundo accounts for about 19 percent, according to HispanTelligence.

McGarrity argues that SiTV and Mun2 will be hampered by the cost of producing original programming as well as securing coveted low-numbered spots on cable dials.

"When people come to Univision, they know they're getting Spanish," McGarrity said. "With SiTV or Mun2, you're in a sea of English competition."

But according to Jeff Valdez, SiTV's co-founder and chairman, Univision isn't the best option for reaching acculturated Hispanics.

Valdez points out that at any given time, roughly 60 percent of Hispanics are watching English-language television while the remainder watch in Spanish, a point backed by a November report from Nielsen Media Research. He said advertisers needed new venues, such as SiTV.

A creator of the groundbreaking Nickelodeon sitcom "The Brothers Garcia," Valdez took seven years, beginning in 1997, to persuade Echostar Communications Corp., operators of the DISH satellite network, and Time Warner Inc. to invest in a Latino-themed, English-language network that would produce its own entertainment.

Now available in more than 7 million homes, SiTV attracts such advertisers as Sears, Verizon Wireless, Suzuki and Wal-Mart.

"This isn't simply about Spanish versus English," he said. "It's about demographics and culture. It's about reaching young people in an environment they can identify with. And that's something new."

Latino Marketing Goes Mainstream

By Samar Farah
The Boston Globe, July 9, 2006

Think back for a moment to this year's Super Bowl—to one commercial that wasn't racy or provocative. In fact, the lack of controversy surrounding this ad is precisely why many advertisers and marketers are still talking about it.

The spot in question promoted a new Toyota Camry Hybrid and featured a father cruising on sun-dappled byways, his son strapped in the back seat. Typical car ad, right? Only the father was a Latino with a discernible accent. Their conversation played on the word hybrid: the son represented a blend of U.S. and Hispanic cultures, the car represented a blend of fuels.

A touching idea, but five years ago, advertising executives say, it would have been unthinkable to blatantly target Hispanics in a mainstream, general market venue such as the Super Bowl. In just 30 seconds, Toyota leapt past two sticking points in corporate marketing departments across the country. The automaker rejected the prevailing wisdom that the only way to connect with Hispanics is in Spanish and through Spanish TV, radio, or print media. Toyota also discredited concerns that prime-time advertising aimed at Hispanics would rankle a non-Hispanic audience; the carmaker says it never heard from any disgruntled viewers.

The Toyota ad "is a milestone in our industry, to say the least," says Alex Lopez Negrete, former chairman of the Association of Hispanic Advertising Agencies and chief executive of Lopez Negrete Communications in Houston.

Toyota is not the only company switching from targeting Hispanics in Spanish to trying to reach Hispanics in English. Last fall Canton sneaker company Reebok created a website in English—BarrioRBK.com—devoted to Hispanic youth, while McDonald's Corp. has been running a TV ad featuring a Latina mother. Shot in both English and Spanish, the fast-food chain's commercial has appeared on high-profile programming including the Oscars and the Grammys in the U.S. Hispanic market.

Most marketers have understood the importance of the Hispanic consumer at least since 2002, when Census figures showed Hispanics surpassed blacks to become the largest minority in the United States.

To that end, brands have spent millions translating their English advertising into Spanish and placing those spots on Spanish-language outlets, from TV to radio. But the majority of Hispanics in America—about 60 percent according to the US Census—are US-born, like the son in the Camry ad. Marketing gurus describe this subset as young, upwardly mobile, tech-savvy, favoring main-stream shows like "American Idol" and "The Simpsons," and either bilingual or else preferring to communicate in English. For the most part, brands have been ignoring this group.

> "Acculturation" is the newest buzzword among multicultural marketers.

Take Evelyn Reyes, 35, producer and host with "Boston Latino," a local cable program in English geared toward Hispanics. Reyes, who was born in New York and grew up in Jamaica Plain, rarely watches Mexican soap operas, or telenovelas, so popular with Hispanics. Aside from visits to her mother's house, where the television set is often tuned to Spanish-language programs, she's unlikely to catch any advertising in Spanish, and she says the same is true of her Hispanic friends.

"We're different from foreign-born Latinos," she says. "I've felt that difference ever since I was a kid. We're more acculturated."

"Acculturation" is the newest buzzword among multicultural marketers. According to the acculturation model, minorities from Latinos to Asian-Americans will blend certain elements of American culture with their own background. Rather than grouping minorities according to language preference and hiring agencies to translate ad copy, marketers who buy into this view are concerned with cultural differences not only between large ethnic categories like Hispanics and Asians, but also between smaller segments like US-born Hispanics and foreign-born Hispanics.

Rick Marroquin, director of Hispanic marketing for McDonald's, explains the fast-food giant's decision to speak to Latinos in English: "We know that Hispanics, regardless of language preference, are more attentive to [marketing] that is culturally relevant. It is a concerted effort to deliver our message to the breadth of Hispanic consumers in the US today."

Toyota has been marketing to Hispanics for about 15 years, but the Super Bowl ad marks its first effort to reach bilingual Hispanics in English, says Sandi Kayse, National Car Advertising Manager for Toyota. While developing the campaign, the company feared a backlash.

"Prior to the ad coming out, we received a small amount of negative feedback saying that we shouldn't use Spanish on English TV stations," Kayse recalls, referring to a bilingual exchange in the father-son conversation using "Si" for "yes."

Kayse said certain facts overrode their concerns: that among Hispanics Toyota is the number one–selling car brand, that the Camry is the number one–selling car in the United States, that Toyota has a firm reputation as a producer of hybrid cars, and that research shows that a significant number of Hispanic Super Bowl viewers care about the environment.

But a gut feeling about the ad's message is what ultimately carried the campaign through. "We wanted to show that [Toyota] is moving forward and that [Hispanics] too are moving forward."

Kayse won't say whether the commercial has translated into more sales among Hispanics but is confident that it has been effective. "It's done more than just highlight a car—it showed that we respect our Hispanic customers and that we're willing to go to the expense of buying a Super Bowl ad to reach them," she said.

Will Toyota try a bilingual ad again? "While we don't have plans to do something similar right now, we certainly realized there are opportunities to cross over diversity media lines," Kayse said.

Liz Cheng, vice president of programming at WCVB-TV, Boston's ABC affiliate, has tried to embrace such opportunities. She said she has made it a priority to reach out to Hispanic viewers through bilingual efforts like Spanish-language captioning and Hispanic programs in English. Cheng sites Census figures that show that Massachusetts's Hispanic population is quickly expanding. From 1990 to 2000, the state's Latino community grew 49 percent.

Even so, Cheng said her sales teams grouse that it's an uphill battle persuading advertisers to shift Hispanic advertising dollars into general market outlets.

"You feel like you're constantly in the process of educating," Cheng said.

Pursuing Hispanic Wealth

By Ben White
The Washington Post, November 26, 2004

The booming Hispanic population is changing American life from pop culture to politics. And investing is no exception.

In research reports and demographic studies, investment firms and business groups are scrambling to identify ways to capitalize on both the exploding size of the Latino population in the United States and expected shifts in consumption patterns. As second- and third-generation Hispanic Americans gain more wealth, they'll begin buying a broader array of goods and services, in banking, housing and health care.

In a study released this week, investment bank Goldman Sachs & Co. noted that Latinos could make up 20 percent of the U.S. population within 25 years and predicted that the income and employment gap between whites and Hispanics will narrow over the same period.

In another report, the Conference Board, a business advisory group, said income among Latinos in the United States could grow by as much as 43 percent over the next six years, to nearly $700 billion by 2010. Other estimates put Latino income in 2010 at closer to $1 trillion.

Both Goldman Sachs and the Conference Board noted that the Latino population is unusually young, with a median age of 25.9 years, according to Census Bureau data, compared with 35.3 years for the broader U.S. population. This means many Latinos have yet to reach their top earning potential, will be spending money longer and are among the age group most coveted by marketers.

As Latino wealth increases, analysts say, Hispanic Americans may begin spending a smaller portion of their income on things like rent, food and clothing and more on financial services, homes, media, health care and other products. Loyalty to traditional Latino brand names could also begin to dissipate as the children of first-generation immigrants become more assimilated into American culture.

"The Hispanic population's growth in size and purchasing power will spill over into industries across the board," said Lynn Franco, director of the Consumer Research Center at the Conference Board. "The numbers are growing exponentially and if you look out beyond 2010, the numbers become just astounding."

In the Goldman Sachs report, analyst David J. Kostin attempted to identify both industries and specific companies that could benefit from the growing purchasing power of Hispanic Americans.

Among others, Kostin cited media companies, home builders and home improvement stores, banks, managed care firms and drugmakers as possible beneficiaries, especially those with a large presence in California, Texas, Florida and New York, the centers of Latino population growth in the United States.

Among specific companies, Kostin listed Belo Corp. and Tribune Co. as media firms with large exposure to the Hispanic market, as well as Univision Communications Inc., the dominant Spanish-language television broadcaster. Belo, which owns the Dallas Morning News among other papers, and Tribune Co., which owns the Los Angeles Times among other newspapers, both have launched Spanish-language efforts.

Media companies in markets with smaller but growing Hispanic populations also have been trying to attract Spanish-language read-

---

"The Hispanic population's growth in size and purchasing power will spill over into industries across the board."—Lynn Franco, director of the Consumer Research Center

---

ers and viewers. The Washington Post Co., for example, recently purchased Arlington-based newsweekly El Tiempo Latino.

Kostin cited General Electric Co., parent company of Spanish-language television network Telemundo, as another possible winner as the Hispanic population grows. But he noted that Telemundo, which captures a far smaller audience than Univision, represents only about 0.3 percent of GE's total annual revenue.

In the consumer products sector, Kostin singled out Avon Products as uniquely positioned because Hispanic women tend to embrace direct home sales of cosmetics more than other demographic groups. Avon earlier this year signed Hispanic actress Salma Hayek as a celebrity spokeswoman for the company.

Among commercial banks, Kostin cited Bank of America and Washington Mutual as firms with the largest market share in California, Florida and Texas and thus the opportunity to benefit from rising incomes among Hispanic Americans.

Kostin said only 51 percent of Latinos in the United States have bank accounts, far below the level for whites and African Americans. However, the numbers are significantly higher for U.S.–born Latinos (58 percent) than for recent immigrants (47 percent), indicating a major opportunity for banks as the population of U.S.–born Latinos rises.

Other big banks beyond Bank of America and Washington Mutual are looking to capitalize on the rising Latino population. Citigroup Inc., the nation's largest financial services firm, recently acquired First American Bank in Texas. And in a September interview, Citigroup chief executive Charles O. Prince III said the firm would continue to look for strategic branch acquisitions in markets such as Texas and Florida.

Kostin, for his part, listed a handful of regional banks that could be targets for acquisition by larger firms, including Compass Bancshares in Texas; City National in California; and Colonial BancGroup in Florida.

Jay C. Garcia, managing director at New York investment bank Samuel A. Ramirez & Co., said financial services is one area where loyalty to Latino-oriented firms such as Puerto Rico–based Banco Popular could diminish over the next decade.

"There is product loyalty, so companies that tailor themselves [to Latinos] should stand to benefit in the short term. But with the second and third generation, they are more mainstream," Garcia said. "They are less likely to embrace the products of the parents or grandparents. . . . So it's going to be less about the Banco Populars of the world and more about the Washington Mutuals."

Despite the anticipated shift in loyalty, Garcia said, companies with largely Hispanic ownership, or that cater to Hispanic customers, are doing remarkably well. In November of last year, Garcia helped launch the Ramirez and Co. Hispanic Index (RCHI), which measures stock performance of the 10 biggest Latino-oriented public companies in the United States and Puerto Rico. The two biggest companies in the index are Banco Popular and Univision.

From August 2000 through November 2003, Garcia calculated that the RCHI rose 124.9 percent, compared with a loss of 7.3 percent for the Dow Jones industrial average and a loss of 26.4 percent for the Standard & Poor's 500-stock index.

V. Education and the Bilingual Debate

Editor's Introduction

The successful integration of Hispanic immigrants and their offspring into American society will depend in large measure on the U.S. educational system. Among the more essential tasks for American educators is English instruction. However, there is considerable disagreement as to the best way to teach the language to non-native speakers. Some argue that a bilingual approach is most effective, that students should be taught in their own languages as well as in English. Others maintain that immersion, or English-only instruction, is the better choice. The debate has become increasingly bitter and fraught with political undertones as immigration skeptics generally promote total immersion while immigration advocates tend toward the bilingual approach. These and other issues surrounding the education of Hispanic Americans are addressed in this chapter.

Despite the strong positions staked out by both sides in the bilingual-immersion debate, recent testing to determine which strategy is more effective has been inconclusive. Kendra Hamilton and Stephen Krashen discuss this situation, as well as the underlying roots of the conflict, in the first article, "Bilingual or Immersion?"

In the next entry, "From the Beginning . . . There Needs to Be Light," Mayra Rodríguez Valladares examines the importance of early education for Hispanic-American children and the economic and social impediments that often prevent them from obtaining instruction.

Given the direct correlation between a quality education and a sound financial future, the state of the public schools attended by Hispanic Americans is of paramount importance. Unfortunately, while most perceive school segregation as a historically black and white issue, Latinos have often been victimized by separate and unequal educational opportunities. In fact, as it is explained in the subsequent piece, "Pew Report: Latinos More Likely than Blacks, Whites to Attend the Largest Public High Schools," from the journal *Diverse Issues in Higher Education*, "Hispanic teens are more likely than Blacks and Whites to attend public high schools that have the most students, the highest concentrations of poor students and highest student-teacher ratios."

Though the Hispanic-American population is booming, there has not been a corresponding increase in Latino college attendance or graduation rates. In fact, the "rates of attendance and graduation remain nearly as low as 20 or 25 years ago," according to Dr. Antonio Flores, as quoted by Garry Boulard in "Demographic Dilemma," the next article in this chapter. Nevertheless, while these rates have not changed, the number of Hispanics entering institutions of higher learning has more than tripled in the past 25 years, notes Peter Schmidt in "Academe's Hispanic Future," the final piece in this section. This increase in Hispanic students has in turn impacted college and university curricula, which have been revised by educators in order to address the needs and interests of Hispanic students.

Bilingual or Immersion?

By Kendra Hamilton and Stephen Krashen
Diverse: Issues in Higher Education, April 20, 2006

Eight years ago, Proposition 227 virtually eliminated bilingual education in California's K–12 schools. Since then, the English-only approach has made inroads in states like Arizona and Massachusetts, where ballot initiatives have created even more restrictive "English immersion" programs than California's. In Colorado, backers of a failed ballot initiative are trying again, this time with a campaign for a constitutional amendment.

But a group of new studies is providing fresh evidence of what many researchers have been saying all along: English immersion has more political appeal than educational merit.

"We're saying it's not possible given the data available to definitively answer the question 'which is better—bilingual or immersion?'" says Dr. Amy Merickel, co-author of "Effects of the Implementation of Proposition 227 on the Education of English Learners K–12". The five-year, $2.5 million study was conducted for the state of California by the American Institutes for Research and WestEd.

"We don't see conclusive evidence that bilingual education is superior to English immersion, and we don't see conclusive evidence for the reverse," Merickel says. "We think it's the wrong question. It's not the model of instruction that matters—it's the quality."

Dr. Tim Shanahan, professor of curriculum and instruction at the University of Illinois–Chicago and director of its Center for Literacy, agrees.

Shanahan and a team of more than a dozen researchers from institutions across the nation recently completed a synthesis of all the available research on literacy, including second language literacy for the U.S. Department of Education.

"When we looked at all the past attempts to get at this issue and analyzed their data, essentially what we concluded was that, in fact, kids did somewhat better if they received some amount of instruction in their home language," Shanahan says. "How much? It was not clear from the available data. What should it look like? That wasn't entirely clear either. But across the board, the impact of some instruction in home language seemed to be beneficial.

"But one of the things that surprised me and that stood out for me was the sheer volume of the research that was not devoted to these issues," he adds. "If you look at the data, most of the research is on [which] language of instruction [is better]. That issue has so sucked up all the oxygen that all those other issues of quality clearly are being neglected."

Such conclusions run sharply counter to the assertions of many defenders of English immersion. In 1997, millionaire Ron Unz began a campaign against bilingual education, forming an advocacy organization with a simple name and message—English for the Children. That organization helped push Proposition 227 to a landslide victory in California, claiming 61 percent of the vote. Two years later, citing dramatic gains on test scores for immigrant children, the English for the Children movement moved to Arizona, where Proposition 203 notched 63 percent of the vote. In 2002, Massachusetts followed suit with Question 2, which was passed with 70 percent support. But in Colorado, voters rejected the English-immersion philosophy, turning it down 55 percent to 44 percent at the polls.

But the movement began to fizzle after 2002. The offices of English for the Children have closed, and studies have consistently been punching holes in core tenets of the English-only argument.

First to fall were the "dramatic gains" in test scores. Proponents of English-immersion stated emphatically that test scores for immigrant students had shot up 40 percent between 1998 and 2000. But research teams from Stanford University, Arizona State University and others pointed out that scores had risen for all students during that period. They also noted that the rising test scores were due to the fact that California had introduced a new achievement test and not to the effects of Proposition 227.

More damning was the failure of Proposition 227 to hold up its central promise. English for the Children had repeatedly claimed that results could be achieved with only a one-year transition period for English learners.

"The one-year limit is a fantasy," says Dr. Stephen Krashen, professor emeritus at the University of Southern California's Rossier School of Education. "In California and Arizona, English learners are currently gaining less than one level per year out of five, where level five means 'ready for the mainstream.'

"That means that a child starting with no English will take at least five years before 'transitioning.' In Massachusetts, after three years of study, only half of the English learners are eligible to be considered for regular instruction," he says.

Merickel's AIR/WestEd research team noted several exemplary programs during the course of their study. Some of the programs were bilingual, others were English immersion and some were "dual immersion"—providing instruction in both Spanish and English.

Prop 227 has actually been a useful tool, she says, for forcing the state to focus much-needed attention on the non–English speaking population. Some former foes of the proposition, she says, "have come to see it as a positive thing."

But Shelly Spiegel-Coleman, president of Californians Together, an advocacy coalition formed in 1998, isn't willing to go so far.

"The truth is Proposition 227 was a horrible blow for us, but if that was all that happened to us since 1998, we could have galvanized attention, made our points" and worked to ease the law's most restrictive elements, she says.

But Prop 227 was the first of a wave of reform movements, each more restrictive than its predecessor. First came a flurry of one-size-fits-all, skill-based reading programs, crafted to meet the curricular needs specified in Prop. 227.

"They allow no accommodation for non-native speakers, and they're sweeping the country," Spiegel-Coleman says.

And then there are the harsh accountability systems mandated by No Child Left Behind.

"There are these people who have so much invested in these English-only reading programs and accountability systems who do not want to admit that what they're doing is wrong for kids," Spiegel-Coleman says.

Indeed, the stakes in these political battles over education could not be higher. According to U.S. Census figures, the number of children living in homes where English is not the primary language more than doubled from 1979 to 1999, from 6 million to 14 million. California was home to more than 1.4 million English learners—or nearly 40 percent of all such public school students in the nation (excluding Puerto Rico).

These "language minority" students face formidable obstacles in school, according to the National Center for Education Statistics. The dropout rate is 31 percent for language minority children who speak English, compared with 51 percent for language minority kids who do not and only 10 percent for the general population.

"At some point," says Shanahan, "we better get serious about immigration, about integrating immigrants as productive, tax-paying and Social Security–supporting parts of our work force. To do these things, they have to be able to do the work that we do in the United States—that means we have to be making quality choices to provide them with a quality education."

But the discussion about quality has only begun, says Shanahan, noting that his review found only 17 studies concerned with educational quality, compared with more than 450 studies examining types of reading programs.

Meanwhile the discussion about the language of instruction—a discussion Shanahan says is deeply political—seems never-ending.

SIX MYTHS ABOUT BILINGUAL EDUCATION

BY DR. STEPHEN KRASHEN

MYTH 1: Bilingual programs are mostly concerned with maintaining the ethnic culture of the family.

RESPONSE: While some bilingual programs encourage development of a student's native language after English has been mastered, the major goal of bilingual education is the rapid acquisition of English and mastery of academic subjects.

MYTH 2: Bilingual education doesn't work; it prevents children from acquiring English.

RESPONSE: Scientific studies consistently show that children in bilingual programs typically score higher on tests of English than do children in all-English immersion programs. In fact, three major reviews coming to this conclusion were published last year in professional, scientific journals.

MYTH 3: Children languish in bilingual programs for many years, never learning enough English to study in mainstream classes.

RESPONSE: According to a recent report from New York City for children entering school at kindergarten and grade 1, only 14 percent were still in bilingual education after six years. From data provided by the state of Texas, I have estimated that for those who started at kindergarten, only 7 percent were still in bilingual education after grade 5.

Most students in bilingual programs in upper grades are those who came to the United States at an older age. These late-comers face a daunting task: Many come with inadequate preparation in their country of origin, and need to acquire English as well as assimilate years of subject matter knowledge.

MYTH 4: Bilingual programs teach only in the native language.

RESPONSE: Some critics have claimed that bilingual education requires that children spend five to seven years mastering their native language before they can learn English. This is not correct. In properly organized bilingual programs, English is introduced immediately. ESL [English as a Second Language instruction] begins from the first day, and subjects are taught in English as soon as they can be made comprehensible. Research confirms that English is not delayed by bilingual education. According to one study of bilingual programs, by the time children are in third grade, 75 percent of their subject matter is in English, and it is 90 percent by grade 5.

MYTH 5: Immigrants, especially Spanish-speakers, are refusing to learn English.

RESPONSE: They aren't refusing to learn English. According to the most recent census, only 7 percent of those who said another language was spoken at home cannot speak English. These figures include newcomers. Census data also tells us that Spanish speakers are acquiring English at the same rate as other groups.

Spanish speakers born in the United States report that they speak, read and write English better than they do Spanish by the time they finish high school. One does, of course, occasionally run into immigrants who don't speak English. These are usually new arrivals, or those who have not been able to find the time or opportunity to acquire English.

MYTH 6: Bilingual education is not done in other countries, only in the United States.

RESPONSE: Bilingual education is not the most widely used approach for children acquiring a second language, but it is widespread. Most European countries provide bilingual education for immigrant children, and studies done by European scholars show that children in these programs acquire the second language of the country as well as and usually better than those in "immersion" programs. There are also numerous programs for the languages spoken by indigenous minority communities. No member of the European Economic Community has passed the equivalent of California's Proposition 227.

From the Beginning . . . There Needs to Be Light

By Mayra Rodríguez Valladares
Hispanic, January/February 2003

Aurora Valladares, a south Texas mother of six, remembers trying to raise her kids in the late 60s and 70s. "Pre-school?" she asks, her dark eyes widening, "I did not know English. I spent all day cooking and cleaning. Where would I find the time to find out about early education programs? How could we afford it?"

The experience of this petite and energetic Mexican immigrant is not one that has improved with time. It repeats itself today among other Latino immigrant parents, in Texas and all across the nation. Lack of knowledge or money prevents thousands of Latino children from ever attending early education programs.

Statistics are staggering. Almost one in five children under the age of 5 in the United States is Latino. And one in three of those Latinos lives below the poverty line. Teachers, experts and community leaders agree that it is almost impossible for Latino children to break the cycle of poverty unless their education starts at a very early age. If it does not, they are already at risk of dropping out of school and destined for a life of low-paying menial jobs. While efforts exist to provide children with early education through programs such as Head Start, the majority of Latino children often do not enter schools until kindergarten or even first grade. By then, they are behind their peers: more so, if they do not speak English.

Economics Cannot Be Ignored

According to research by Bowling Green State University's professors Jenny van Hook and Kelly Stamper Balistreri, Hispanics in California present a clear example of what happens to Latino children all across the country. Because "they are the largest immigrant group and tend to be poor and to be residentially segregated . . . it is nearly impossible for school districts in Hispanic areas not to be mostly poor, mostly minority, and mostly non-English-speaking."

They add that these problems have led scholars in the field of education of immigrants to argue that schools in these poor and residentially segregated neighborhoods "produce inequality rather than equalize opportunity." This is particularly grave for small children. The authors found that California children who attend "low-status,

MAKING LEARNING COME ALIVE . . .

Lizann Cruz-Hinds, a Cuban-American entrepreneur, would sit in front of the television with her little girl and would simultaneously interpret English educational programs into Spanish. She would encourage her small daughter to repeat words in English and Spanish. In observing this, her husband, Rick Hinds, suggested that they should start a company that sold bilingual interactive videos and books. This was the start of Fun With Languages.

Fun With Languages focuses on the newborn to 5-year-old segment. The company's educational videos, DVDs, and books have been very well received by parents, grandparents, and educators. In addition, "parents who have children with disabilities have found using our products very useful even when children are older than five." Once they decided to form the company the Hindses researched the market and found practically nothing like what they had in mind. "We saw things in English or Spanish, but not in both." Cruz-Hinds recalls. The company now has bilingual products in English, Spanish, French and Portuguese. The "videos are interactive. Parents get very involved. We also include classical music to stimulate children's brains."

Cruz-Hinds and her husband are strong believers that children can learn a lot, especially in the early years. "A child's mind is like a window letting everything come in. By the time they are between 5 and 8, the window closes." Children continue to learn, but not at the speed at which they can in those early years. For more information, visit www.funwithlanguages.com.

high-minority schools learn less than children who attend integrated schools," particularly in schools where the concentration of minority students is prevalent.

Education Has to Begin Early

"At pre-school age is when children can learn the most. They are like sponges!" explains Sugatha Alladi, an experienced teacher of children between the ages of 2 to 6 at a Montessori school in Somerset, New Jersey.

Ynes Cruz, who taught kindergarten to eighth grade students for 34 years in Dade County in Florida, contends that in kindergarten it was immediately evident who had been to pre-school or not. "Children who went to pre-school had an advantage," recalls Cruz. "They came with English, had the ability to manage pencils and paper, and were already adapted to a school environment."

She found that the children who had not been in pre-school programs took a long time to adjust to being in the kindergarten. "The difference was still noticeable in the first grade. If a child had a high IQ and had a rich learning environment at home, then they could catch up. Most of the time, however, this does not take place. About 75 percent of the children who had not attended pre-school carried that disadvantage for a long time."

According to Early Child Initiative Foundation's Chief Operating Officer Ana Sejeck, "if a kid has a good caregiver who is dedicated to taking them to all sorts of things, like libraries, music programs, and settings for children to interact with each other, then the child will probably succeed as well as his/her peers who have been to a pre-school program. Unfortunately, reality is that most parents have to work and hence cannot give children structured education and stimulus." Consequently, "a child with no early education is already at a disadvantage in the first grade. Parents need to understand that children have to be read to, that they have to play with other children, be fed properly, and they have to have health care."

Parents' Education and Financial Status Are Critical

The reasons why Latino children do not attend early education programs are numerous. "Pre-school (in Florida) is usually not free," Cruz says. "In Dade County, some of these programs can cost $65–$100 a week. For some families, especially if they have more than one child of pre-school age, those fees are unaffordable." When it comes to private school pre-school education, the cost can be prohibitive. In New York, Alicia Meléndez, a Puerto Rican mother, paid

---

ART AND LITERACY

Elba Montalvo, head of the Commission for Hispanic Families and Children (CHFC) in New York, believes that cultural differences have a tremendous influence on parents and how they relate to their children's education, starting in preschool. "Schools do not know how to engage parents, how to make them feel welcome," she explains. "Often parents do not know how to participate in the U.S. education system. In the old country you dropped your kids off at school and that was it. Here expectations for parents are different."

In the U.S., parents are children's advocates. Latino parents tend not to be advocates and "assume that children are being taken care of in school. Parents place an enormous faith in schools," explained Montalvo, a successful Puerto Rican educator and administrator. She emphasizes that "parents have to be a part of every effort to educate children."

CHFC runs an eight-week after-school program on Saturdays for parents and second and third grade children. Teachers and parents encourage their children to write stories and to drawl accompanying illustrations. The program requires children to read at least for 20 minutes at home. Some parents who do not speak English "felt that this was a useless exercise," explains Montalvo, "yet the school has made the parents feel welcome at school meetings and events and has proven to these paretns that disciplining children to read can make a difference."

over $8,000 a year, or $211 a week, for her son Paulo to attend a private school for a 38-week, four hours a day program. "Had I wanted to send him more hours," explains Meléndez, "it would have been even costlier."

Significant lack of knowledge about early education also exists. Parents often confuse daycare centers for pre-school. "Child care is not necessarily pre-school, and even some pre-schools are not teaching children anything," says Alladi. "A good pre-school is one with a solid curriculum." Sejeck agrees. "Often child-care centers are not accredited. In Dade County, there are 1,400 licensed day care centers, but only 106 are accredited," Sejeck explained. "I did not know when I was putting my kids in day care, that there is a big difference (between programs). Now I say to parents, 'Do not just warehouse your children in a center.'"

Cultural issues also affect parental attitudes about such programs. Dr. Linda Espinosa, co-director of the National Institute for Early Education Research (NIEER) in New Brunswick, New Jersey, contends that early education programs "need to make a concerted effort to make families comfortable; otherwise, families feel alienated." Word of mouth reputation is what sells or destroys a program. "We made our program family friendly." The program now has a long waiting list.

According to Espinosa, Latino families have a very difficult time "letting go of their 3-year-olds to strangers who often speak another language and come from a different culture. Anglo middle-class families, on the other hand, accept that kids need to go to pre-school to get socialized." There is much to be done to convince the parents of Hispanic children of the benefits of pre-school programs and of the adverse consequences of a late start in school.

Head Start Makes a Good Effort, but the Majority of Latinos Are Not Covered

Head Start, a national program created in 1965, provides early education to children under 5. Dr. Wade Horn, Director of the Administration for Children and Families at the U.S. Department of Health and Human Services, explains that each of his department's programs "help provide services to the most vulnerable children. Clearly economic disadvantage causes vulnerability. Disproportionately, Hispanic children are poor, so as a matter of course we provide services to them." He also stated that "in some areas we have specific outreach (programs) for Hispanic children. In others, we cover them through our regular programs that target lower income families and children."

Head Start also runs a program for migrants, which covers 37,000. Many, if not most of them, are Latino. Providing for migrants is a "unique challenge because families are moving according to agricultural cycles." Head Start has made an effort to model some programs to try to serve these children. "One is a program that moves with families as they move for agricultural opportunities. The other model is one where centers (are placed) in areas where migrant families might live."

The Administration for Families and Children recognizes the need to carry out specific outreach for Hispanics. Horn states that the Administration is involved "in public education and invariably in English and Spanish public service announcements." The Administration has also had Hispanic forums about child support issues and has tried to reach out to Hispanic media. He admits, however, that despite the Administration's best intentions, more effort needs to focus on reaching Latino families and children.

While the Latinos served by Head Start constitute 30 percent of all the children in the program, they only represent 19 percent of the 1.2 million poor Latino children who need to be covered. This means that 80 percent of Latino children who also cannot afford any other kind of early education programs are not going to school until they are 5 or 6 years old, by which time their peers have had exposure to the English language, engaging in educational activities, and interacting with children outside their families.

SETTING UP A BILINGUAL PRE-SCHOOL PROGRAM IN NEW YORK

Jennifer Weiss Friedman and Jennifer Woodruff started looking at pre-schools before their children were 1-year-old. They wanted Jack and Dora to be bilingual in Spanish and English. From their experience as educators, they were convinced that if they begin early, children learn a second language with great ease. But Friedman and Woodruff were shocked to find that while there are French and Italian pre-schools in Manhattan, there were no pre-school with a curriculum specifically designed to teach children in Spanish and English. They took matters into their own hands and founded La Escuelita.

According to Weiss Friedman, "children learn through play, through real-life experiences, and through teacher-guided activities." Thus La Escuelita focuses on subjects in "Spanish and English language development as well as other content areas such as math and literacy. We also incorporate science and social studies into daily activities. For example, a cooking activity can incorporate science (seeing the ingredients change from solid to liquid as it melts), math (measuring), social studies (learning about the culture of the kind of food being prepared) and literacy (identifying letters on a recipe or hearing a book about the food being prepared)."

La Escuelita's directors are strong proponents of early education. "Early education has wonderful implications for learning and development." These educators are also strong proponents of properly taught bilingual education. "As a speech-language pathologist. I have seen from experience and from the research the wonderful benefits of bilingualism. The key is supporting both languages." Research into bilingual education programs in New York Public Schools show that children in dual language programs end up out performing other children on formal testing. They end up with stronger Spanish and English skills. "By supporting literacy and learning in both languages, the children become highly educated bilingual adults!" Weiss Friedman said.

Pew Report: Latinos More Likely than Blacks, Whites to Attend the Largest Public High Schools

DIVERSE: ISSUES IN HIGHER EDUCATION, NOVEMBER 17, 2005

Hispanic teens are more likely than Blacks and Whites to attend public high schools that have the most students, the highest concentrations of poor students and highest student-teacher ratios, according to a new Pew Hispanic Center analysis. The findings came in one of three studies released earlier this month by the center that examined youths in high schools and colleges.

The report found that more than half of Latinos (56 percent) attend the nation's largest public high schools—those schools whose enrollment size ranks them in the 90th percentile or higher. That's compared with 32 percent of Blacks and 26 percent of Whites.

The report also found that about 37 percent of Latinos attend the 10 percent of schools with the highest student-teacher ratios. Just 14 percent of Black students and 13 percent of Whites attend those schools, which have a student-teacher ratio greater than 22-to-1, compared with the national average of 16-to-1.

While much of the research on the achievement gap between Hispanics and Whites has focused on student characteristics, the new study examines the structural characteristics of the high schools attended by different racial and ethnic groups.

"The characteristics of high schools matter for student performance," says Dr. Richard Fry, senior research associate at the center and the author of the three reports. "Hispanic teens are more likely than any other racial or ethnic group to attend public high schools that have the dual characteristics of extreme size and poverty."

A second report released by the center on the high school attendance of foreign-born teens points to the importance of schooling abroad in understanding the dropout problem for immigrant teens. The report found that immigrant dropouts had already fallen behind in their education before coming to the United States. Immigrant teens contribute disproportionately to the overall number of the nation's dropouts, often calculated as the number of school-aged teens not enrolled in school.

In a third report, the center found that the number of young Hispanics going to college is increasing. But the study, which examined the latest available enrollment data from individual colleges, found that the number of Whites enrolling in four-year colleges is increasing even more rapidly—widening an already large gap between White and Latino college populations in key states. "When it comes to college enrollment, Hispanics are chasing a target that is accelerating ahead of them," Fry says.

KEY FINDINGS FROM THE THREE REPORTS:

- One-in-four Hispanic high school students attends one of the 300 public high schools that are in the top decile in size of student enrollment and also have a high proportion of students eligible for free or reduced-price school lunches. That's compared with fewer than 1-in-10 Black students and just 1-in-100 White students.

- Only 8 percent of the nation's teens are foreign-born, but nearly 25 percent of teen dropouts are foreign-born. Nearly 40 percent of these foreign-born dropouts are recent arrivals who interrupted their schooling before coming to the United States.

- Nationally, there was a 24 percent increase in the number of Latino freshmen in postsecondary institutions in 2001 compared with 1996. Among four-year colleges, Latino freshmen enrollment increased by 29 percent while two-year colleges experienced a 14 percent increase.

Demographic Dilemma

By Garry Boulard
Diverse: Issues in Higher Education, January 26, 2006

Educators and policymakers are worried that despite a growing population, Hispanic college attendance and graduation rates haven't changed in 20 years.

As he enters his last semester of law school at the University of New Mexico, Diego Esquibel remains convinced that he probably would not be where he is today had it not been for the unwavering support of his parents, who repeatedly insisted that he complete his formal education.

"Their thinking has always been that if I did not stick with it and instead went off in some other direction, I would essentially be closing doors for myself that should be open," says Esquibel. "So sometimes, more for them than even for me, I have continued on. And now that I am so near to the end, I am really glad that I did."

This year, Esquibel, 28, will not only be wrapping up his studies at UNM but also working in the local district attorney's office in Albuquerque. He hopes the job will help him get a feel for the daily life of a public prosecutor.

But although he comes from a university with a growing percentage of Hispanic students, Esquibel is still more of the exception than the norm, especially when it comes to the graduate and professional schools.

"It is true that there are not as many Latino students at that level of education as we would like to see," says Raul Gonzalez, education policy analyst with the National Council of La Raza, a Hispanic civil rights and advocacy organization. "That remains so across the board, in two-year schools, four-year schools and in graduate schools. It has been a problem that has been going on for a very long time."

For educators and policymakers, the problem is particularly challenging because the lag has taken place during a time of dramatic growth in the country's overall Hispanic population. Hispanics now comprise 14 percent of the national population, and their numbers are growing faster than any other demographic group. Many demographers believe the number will rise to 18 percent by 2020.

Ten-Year Changes in Hispanic Master's Degree Disciplines

Master's Degrees	Number of Degrees			Representation (Pct. of Total)		
	1994	2004	% Chg.	1994	2004	% Chg.
Education and Human Services	4,454	12,123	172%	3.6%	6.1%	2.5%
Social and Behavioral Sciences	905	1,733	91%	3.4%	5.1%	1.7%
Humanities and Fine Arts	978	1,634	67%	3.4%	4.7%	1.3%
Health Professions	690	2,044	196%	2.4%	4.5%	2.1%
Other Professions	587	1,268	116%	2.3%	4.2%	1.9%
Business	2,390	5,450	128%	2.6%	3.9%	1.4%
Science, Tech, Engineering and Math	1,117	2,114	89%	2.0%	2.9%	0.9%
Agricultural Sciences	182	108	-41%	4.4%	2.3%	-2.2%
Total	**11,303**	**26,474**	**134%**	**2.9%**	**4.7%**	**1.8%**

Source: *Black Issues In Higher Education*, Top 100 Graduate Edition, July 14, 2005

As a result, says Dr. Antonio Flores, the president and CEO of the Hispanic Association of Colleges and Universities, "There are more Hispanics emerging into all levels of education by virtue of the sheer explosive Hispanic population growth, but their rates of attendance and graduation remain nearly as low as 20 or 25 years ago."

According to HACU's most recent data, there were just more than 1.7 million Hispanic students enrolled in some form of higher education in 2004. The number represents just 7 percent of all postsecondary education students. The picture is even more troubling at the graduate level, where Hispanics comprise only 6.2 percent of the population. Only about 10 percent of Hispanic undergraduate students continue on to graduate school, which is leading some policymakers to suspect a problem with the pipeline.

Says Gonzalez, "A very large number of Latino students who make it to a four-year school are often the first in the family to do so, which means they do not possess the level of sophistication that comes when you are a second- or third-generation college-goer who knows what to expect at the four-year level and is already making plans for graduate school when they enter undergraduate school."

The Power of Culture

The percentage of Hispanic students is even lower in the nation's medical schools.

"About 5 percent of all medical students and residents in the country today are of Hispanic origin," says Dr. Elena Rios, president and CEO of the National Hispanic Medical Association.

"That is very obviously a number that is significantly lower than the general population, enough so that I don't think we are ever going to catch up in terms of representing the general population," she says.

The fact that more Hispanic females than males are currently attending the nation's medical schools may present an entirely different problem. Hispanic communities nationwide may find themselves confronted with a distinct shortage of male Hispanic physicians.

"This is really a very powerful reflection of culture," says Rios, who recently attended a conference at Stanford University that attracted nearly 30 Hispanic pre-med students, only one of whom was male.

"The pressure for a Hispanic male student to get out of school quickly and get married or go to work and help with the family is far greater than anyone who is not a part of that world can imagine," Rios says, adding that for every student like Esquibel whose parents insisted that he complete school, there are at least one or two other Hispanic students with families who do not view attending college as an important priority.

"It is almost as if you have to go against your own family if you are expected to have any chance at all of making it to college, much less to graduate school," she says.

Learning a new language is just one more obstacle for many Hispanic elementary and high school students. That challenge is made all the more difficult because large numbers of Hispanic students attend impoverished inner-city public schools.

"These kinds of hurdles can defeat some kids early on, making it almost impossible for them to think of finishing high school or going to college later on," says Melissa Lazarin, education and policy analyst with the National Council of La Raza.

Ten-Year Changes in Hispanic Doctoral Degree Disciplines

Doctoral Degrees	Number of Degrees			Representation (Pct. of Total)		
	1994	2004	% Chg.	1994	2004	% Chg.
Social and Behavioral Sciences	208	402	93%	2.8%	4.7%	1.8%
Education and Human Services	208	326	57%	2.7%	4.1%	1.3%
Humanities and Fine Arts	127	197	55%	2.9%	3.7%	0.8%
Health Professions	25	138	452%	1.3%	3.2%	1.9%
Business	13	44	238%	0.9%	3.0%	2.1%
Other Professions	38	59	55%	1.4%	2.5%	1.0%
Science, Tech, Engineering and Math	237	373	57%	1.4%	2.2%	0.8%
Agricultural Sciences	18	18	0%	1.4%	1.5%	0.1%
Total	**874**	**1,557**	**78%**	**2.0%**	**3.2%**	**1.2%**

Source: *Black Issues In Higher Education*, Top 100 Graduate Edition, July 14, 2005

Says Rios, "It all comes back to the pipeline, of students getting from one level of school to another, but somehow instead falling by the wayside because they don't have the kind of role models they need or are lacking for family support when it comes to this particular kind of pursuit."

But despite the challenges, the numbers of Hispanic graduate students are slowly rising at some schools, due in large part to extensive recruitment efforts at those institutions.

"Schools have to do whatever they can to get the word out," says Eric Abrams, the director of diversity initiatives at Stanford's Graduate School of Business. "If you fail to do that, it is kind of hard at the end of the day to see an increase in the numbers of whatever group it is you are targeting."

Stanford has partnered with organizations such as the National Association of Hispanic MBAs and the Society of Professional Engineers to help increase the number of Hispanic students in its graduate programs. The university has launched a series of informational sessions throughout the Western Hemisphere to garner interest among Hispanic students.

"Just this last year alone I was in Lima [Peru], Caracas [Venezuela] and Bogotá [Colombia], while others in our office have been to Mexico City, Monterrey and Montevideo, not to mention a number of cities around this country," says Abrams. "We never wait for anyone to come to our doors."

Such efforts have yielded results. Hispanic students currently make up 100 of the 753 students enrolled in Stanford's business school, a number officials say has remained fairly steady the last few years.

"These are not huge numbers, admittedly," he says. "But the very fact that we are out in the community making our presence known sends a powerful signal that this really is something important to us. And I think that sort of thing has a funny way of influencing not only which school a student ultimately decides to go to, but also whether or not a student even wants to go to graduate school in the first place."

Multiple Approaches

While Stanford is traveling the globe searching out Hispanic students, many other schools are attempting to boost their Hispanic populations via more traditional methods, including well-established international student programs.

This fall, officials with the University of Arizona's Graduate College announced that they were expanding a 25-year-old agreement with Mexico's Consejo Nacional de Ciencia y Tecnologia (Conacyt) program. The expanded program will jointly fund the education of up to 100 doctoral students from Mexico, a significant increase from the 20 students funded in previous years.

Ten-Year Changes in Hispanic First Professional Degree Disciplines

First Professional Degrees	Number of Degrees			Representation (Pct. of Total)		
	1994	2004	% Chg.	1994	2004	% Chg.
Law	1,792	2,273	27%	4.3%	5.7%	1.3%
Medicine	596	757	27%	3.9%	4.9%	1.0%
Dentistry	211	193	-9%	5.6%	4.5%	-1.1%
Other Medicine/Health	348	684	97%	3.4%	3.9%	0.5%
Divinity	111	136	23%	1.8%	2.6%	0.8%
Total	**3,058**	**4,043**	**32%**	**4.0%**	**4.9%**	**0.9%**

Source: *Black Issues In Higher Education*, Top 100 Graduate Edition, July 14, 2005

"Some time ago, our university made the decision that it wanted to increase the number of Hispanic students in its graduate enrollments and that it would look to Mexico and Central America as excellent places for making that possible," says Dr. Maria Teresa Velez, associate dean of UA's graduate college.

In addition to the agreement with Conacyt, UA is also seeing a surge of American Hispanic students, particularly in the university's science departments, says Velez.

"There were only about 20 students of Hispanic origin in the biomedical sciences as recently as five years ago," she says. "But now that number is right around 50."

In Albuquerque, the University of New Mexico has recruited closer to home, drawing from a growing pool in a city and state where the overall Hispanic population tops 42 percent.

That approach appears to be working. Hispanics accounted for 169 of the 1,000 total graduate students in UNM's spring graduation. The figure represents almost 17 percent of the university's total graduate student enrollment.

With an 18 percent undergraduate enrollment, Hispanic students are expected to continue matriculating through UNM's graduate programs in the near future, say college officials.

"That is how it is going to be almost everywhere," says Lazarin of the National Council of La Raza. "The fastest-growing segment of today's Latino population is in the under-18 category, which means that we can expect to see much larger numbers of Latino students in the next decade or so, not only in undergraduate schools, but graduate schools as well."

Such an increase might serve to compensate for the recent decline in Hispanic students. Although the U.S. Supreme Court ruled that race was a valid academic admissions criteria in the 2003 *Grutter v. Bollinger* case, many schools and graduate pipeline programs such as the Ford Foundation Diversity Fellows program and the Mellon

Mays Undergraduate Fellowship have changed their names and modified their eligibility requirements in an attempt to make them less specific to any one race or ethnic group.

"The fact that schools have been getting rid of racially exclusive programs does not mean that there will be fewer Latinos at the undergraduate and graduate levels," says Roger Clegg, president and general counsel for the Center for Equal Opportunity. "That is primarily so because there is going to be a bigger pool of Hispanic students in general over the next few years. Even without the pipeline programs, their numbers are all slated to increase."

But even a rapid increase won't close the enrollment gap between Hispanics and other graduate students, says Rios. She contends that medical, law and business associations must take it upon themselves to target Hispanic students if they hope to narrow the gap.

"This is not something that we can rely on the government to do or expect the schools to do all by themselves," she says. "The professions themselves have to get involved with their own kind of strategic vision. And until that happens, I think the gap is going to remain. It may get somewhat smaller—but it is not going to disappear any time soon."

Academe's Hispanic Future

By Peter Schmidt
The Chronicle of Higher Education, November 28, 2003

If they haven't already, college professors and administrators should try to get accustomed to pronouncing names like Alejandro, Jorge, Nuria, and Pilar.

Hispanics have become the largest minority group in the United States and now represent about 13 percent of the country's population. They account for about half of the population growth in recent years and are expected, given immigration and their relatively high fertility rates, to represent a much larger share of the population and work force in years to come. Of the 5.6 million additional school-age children projected to be living in the United States in 2025, some 5.2 million, or 93 percent, will be Hispanic, the U.S. Census Bureau says.

Along with growing rapidly, the nation's Hispanic population is spreading out, quickly moving into communities in the South and Midwest where few Hispanics had settled before.

As they show up on campuses, Hispanic students are having a profound influence from the Mexican border to Minnesota, from California to the Carolinas.

In the past decade more than 240 colleges have been designated "Hispanic-serving institutions" by the federal government, meaning that at least a quarter of their enrollment is Hispanic and more than half of their students come from low-income backgrounds. While 49 of the institutions are in Puerto Rico, California has 73; Texas, 38; New Mexico, 20; and Arizona, Florida, Illinois, and New York each have at least 10. Others are located in Colorado, Massachusetts, New Jersey, Oklahoma, Oregon, and Washington. The list grows by about a half-dozen colleges each year.

"Relatively speaking, we are the newest kid on the higher-education block," says Antonio R. Flores, president of the Hispanic Association of Colleges and Universities, which represents Hispanic-serving institutions.

The federal government did not classify colleges as "Hispanic-serving" until 1992. By contrast, historically black colleges and universities date back to 1837. Now some Hispanic-serving institutions, especially in Texas, have such large Hispanic enrollments that they are seeking to make the education of those students a key part of their mission and identity, and they are looking to historically black colleges and universities as potential models, Mr. Flores says.

Many other colleges are establishing new courses geared toward Hispanic students; aggressively trying to recruit Hispanic students, faculty members, and administrators; and overhauling their admissions practices and student services to be more attentive to Hispanic needs. Meanwhile, the Bush administration says it is committed to helping more Hispanics get into college.

"Black and White Paradigm"

There is still plenty of room for improvement. Hispanic students remain severely underrepresented and underserved in higher education.

Colleges have made some progress. Since 1980, the number of Hispanics enrolled in colleges has more than tripled, to nearly 1.5 million, outpacing the rate of Hispanic population growth, which has more than doubled to about 38.8 million. Hispanics' share of all bachelor's degrees awarded has risen from about 2.3 percent to about 6.2 percent.

But though Hispanics represent about 18 percent of the college-age population, they account for just 9.5 percent of all students at the nation's higher-education institutions, and just 6.6 percent of enrollments at four-year colleges.

Over all, Hispanics are the least-educated major racial or ethnic group. Just 11 percent of those over the age of 25 have a bachelor's degree, compared with about 17 percent of black, 27 percent of white, and 47 percent of Asian-American adults in the same age bracket. More than two-fifths of Hispanic adults over 25 never graduated from high school, and more than one-fourth have less than a ninth-grade education.

In terms of overall Hispanic educational attainment, "we were doing better in the '70s than we are in the 21st century," says Raul Yzaguirre, president of the National Council of La Raza, one of the nation's largest Hispanic-advocacy groups.

In many parts of the country, colleges' efforts to serve minority populations remain focused almost solely on black students, even where local Hispanic populations are burgeoning.

In Atlanta, the Hispanic population increased nearly tenfold, to about 290,000, during the 1990s. But Hispanics account for just a dozen of the 1,900 students enrolled at Atlanta Metropolitan College, which has a 95-percent-black student body. Harold E. Wade, the college's president, says predominantly Hispanic neighborhoods have cropped up "within walking distance" of his two-year public institution, but "a lot of Hispanic youngsters who have migrated into this area have not reached college age yet," and their parents don't enroll because they "have come here to work and to take care of families here and in Mexico."

Throughout the nation, "we are still seeing education through a black and white paradigm," Mr. Yzaguirre says. Hispanic students, he says, "are not being given the proper priority."

Hispanic men remain especially underserved. A report issued by the American Council on Education last month found that between the late 1970s and the late 1990s, the college-participation rate for Hispanic men remained essentially unchanged, at 31 percent. For Hispanic women, the college-participation rate increased from 27 percent to 37 percent.

Swimming Against the Tide

Several trends in higher education may be making it even harder for Hispanics to get a college education:

- Last year loans accounted for nearly 70 percent of all federal financial assistance available to college students, up from about 56 percent two decades ago. Raymund A. Paredes, vice president for programs at the Hispanic Scholarship Fund, the nation's largest private provider of scholarships to Hispanic students, says the shift from grants to loans "is having a very serious impact on the Latino community," which is relatively poor and leery of taking on debt. Many more Hispanics would be attending college if they could get grants rather than loans, and many more would pursue advanced degrees "if they could get out from under this debt that they incur as undergraduates," he says.

- Given their relatively high rate of poverty, Hispanic students have been hit hard by the stiff increases in public-college tuition and the cuts in state financial aid that have come in recent years.

- Because many Hispanics inhabit the nation's fastest-growing regions (and are driving much of that growth), they are especially likely to live near colleges that have been resorting to enrollment caps to hold down costs. They are also disproportionately likely to be turned away when colleges raise their admissions standards to curtail enrollment growth or bolster their own reputations, since the standardized-test scores of Hispanics tend to be significantly lower than those of whites.

- Legal and political assaults on affirmative action may also be taking a toll on Hispanic enrollment. Wherever selective colleges have been forced to limit or abandon their use of race- and ethnicity-conscious admissions, the result has been an immediate drop in the share of Hispanic applicants they accept. Hispanic enrollment has rebounded somewhat when colleges have aggressively used alternatives to affirmative action, such as considering socioeconomic status or automatically admitting those near the top of their high-school classes. But the effectiveness of such policies toward ensuring Hispanic access, especially in graduate and professional schools, remains in dispute.

In the past two years, legal challenges have also been mounted against scholarship, internship, and academic-support programs reserved specifically for minority students. Several colleges have either abandoned the programs or opened them up to all races and ethnicities, based on their lawyers' advice that the programs are legally vulnerable.

Leaks in the Pipeline

Policy analysts often speak of the various sectors of education as pieces of a pipeline. At every stage of that pipeline, Hispanic students are getting stuck or spilling out.

Their problems begin in their early years, when many Hispanic children receive little exposure to English, and they are much likelier than white children and nearly as likely as black children to be living in poverty. Several studies have shown that the schools they enter tend to be some of the nation's most segregated and poorly financed, and are more likely than others to be staffed by teachers with little experience in their fields.

By the age of 17, Hispanic high-school students, on average, have the same reading and mathematics skills as white 13-year-olds. More than a third of the states recently surveyed by the National

---

By the age of 17, Hispanic high-school students, on average, have the same reading and mathematics skills as white 13-year-olds.

Center for Education Statistics said that their Hispanic students were significantly more likely than others to drop out of school. And those who earned their diplomas were less likely than their white peers to have taken rigorous college-preparatory courses such as Algebra II and chemistry, according to a report issued last month by the Education Trust, a nonprofit research and advocacy organization based in Washington, D.C.

"The curriculum matters hugely," says Paul Ruiz, one of the Education Trust's chief researchers. "A robust curriculum is the single greatest predictor of college success."

It is not that Hispanic families fail to see the value of education. Family surveys conducted by the Education Department show that more than 9 out of 10 Hispanic parents expect their children to attend college—a figure in line with the results for both black and white parents. But Hispanic children are much less likely than white children to have a parent who attended college.

"It is absolutely the case that they have parental support, but they don't have anybody in the family who really knows the ropes," says Tomás A. Arciniega, president of California State University at Bakersfield, which has an enrollment that is about 36 percent Hispanic, and serves the children of many Mexican and Central American migrant workers employed by local farms and food-processing plants. Like many colleges, his institution is collaborating with the local community-college district and public schools to try to get more Hispanic children to go on to college.

The educational problems of Hispanic Americans don't end at the college door. Hispanic freshmen are less likely than white students to progress to upper-division courses, and Hispanic students who make it to their third year of college are less likely to earn bachelor's degrees, according to the Inter-University Program for Latino Research, a national consortium of 18 Hispanic-focused research centers.

On the whole, Hispanic students are far likelier than white students to be enrolled in two-year colleges, to be working to support themselves or their families, or attending college part time—choices that they often can't help making but that reduce their chances of ever earning bachelor's or advanced degrees.

"The biggest challenge that these kids have to face is, How do they balance what they see as their responsibility to help out at home now that they are young adults and, at the same time, follow their dream of going on to college?" says Mr. Arciniega. He routinely urges faculty and staff members to sit down with students who also work and convince them of how much more money they will earn in a lifetime with a degree.

"We are constantly hitting on the note that college is important," he says.

Only black students have a worse college-graduation rate than Hispanics, and Hispanics have the lowest rate of graduate-school enrollment of any major racial and ethnic group. At the very end of the educational pipeline, Hispanics earn just 4 percent of the doctorates awarded by colleges. A report issued last month by the American Council on Education says that the number of Hispanics earning doctorates or professional degrees actually declined slightly in recent years.

Those statistics help explain why Hispanics account for just 2.9 percent of full-time college faculty members and just 3.2 percent of college administrators.

Repairs in just a few segments of the education pipeline could produce significant increases in the number of Hispanics earning degrees, according to the Inter-University Program for Latino Research. In a 2001 report, it crunched the numbers and determined that if Hispanic high-school students earned their diplomas and went on to four-year colleges at the same rate as white students, the result—all other things remaining equal—would be a 25-percent increase in the number who earn bachelor's degrees each year. Increases of 12 percent in the number of baccalaureates annually awarded to Hispanics could be produced by ensuring that those in two-year colleges transfer to four-year colleges at the same rate as white students, or by ensuring that those who are freshmen at four-year colleges graduate at the same rate as white students.

Among the institutions that have mounted concerted efforts to retain Hispanic students is Lehman College of the City University of New York system, which has about a 47-percent Hispanic enrollment. It operates a program that keeps freshmen together in groups of 25 to 30 to provide one another with support. The faculty members involved share information about particular students and seek to integrate the curriculums of their respective classes so that students in an English-composition class can be working on assignments that they can turn in to their sociology professor.

"This program is costly because you have to pay faculty for additional hours of meetings with each other and with students," Ricardo R. Fernandez, president of Lehman College, says. But, he says, "the students like it," and he is confident that the program keeps many from dropping out during their crucial first year.

St. Philip's College, a public two-year institution in San Antonio, Tex., has the distinction of being classified as both historically black and Hispanic-serving, with an enrollment that is about a fifth black and half Hispanic. Angie S. Runnels, its president, says Hispanic students there clearly benefit from support services developed for black students, such as tutoring programs; instructional laboratories focused on reading, writing, and mathematics; and an approach to student advising that disperses counselors into academic divisions and departments to ensure adequate guidance.

"We are particularly interested in students who are the first generation in their families to experience college," Ms. Runnels says.

Partly because they offer night classes and training for specific jobs, the nation's for-profit colleges have proved especially adept at recruiting and retaining Hispanic students, even though they often charge more than public higher-education institutions.

Many experts on Hispanic college students believe that their educational attainment would improve, especially in graduate and professional schools, if they were more willing to travel long distances to colleges well suited to meet their needs. "An emphasis on close family ties is one characteristic shared by most Latinos regardless of national origin or income, and among Latino immigrants this often translates into an expectation that children will live with their parents until they marry," says a report by the Pew Hispanic Center.

A Diverse Group

Despite their linguistic and cultural similarities, the nation's Hispanic residents are very diverse. Experts on educating them generally agree that getting a larger proportion through college will require focusing on educational differences that the collective term "Hispanic" now masks.

For instance, Cuban-Americans ages 18 to 24 are slightly more likely than white students their age to be enrolled in college, and 90 percent attend full time, more than any other racial or ethnic group. They are also about as likely as white students to go on to graduate school. In contrast, Mexican-American students in that age bracket are about half as likely as their Puerto Rican or Cuban-American peers to be attending two-year colleges.

Puerto Ricans, many of whom travel back to the island often or for extended periods, as family or work needs dictate, can have distinct educational needs tied to their mobility. "You can have a kid who will start in Puerto Rico in September and be in New York in November," says Felix V. Matos Rodriguez, director of the Center for Puerto Rican Studies at Hunter College.

"It all depends on what circumstances they come here for," says Eduardo J. Padrón, president of Miami Dade College, where the enrollment is two-thirds Hispanic. "If they come here as a result of political circumstances, what you find is that some of them are better prepared than our native students. If the immigration is economic immigration, what you find is that most of these people come with a lack of knowledge of the culture and language. Even in their own language, they are not well prepared."

It also matters greatly whether Hispanic students or their parents were born in the United States or abroad.

Statistics that represent Hispanics as a group often are severely skewed by the foreign-born, who account for about 40 percent of the overall Hispanic population. One example: On average, Hispanic males 25 and older have 10.6 years of schooling. When immigrants are taken out of the equation, however, Hispanics' educational attainment rises to 12 years.

> The educational prospects improve substantially for the U.S.–born children of Hispanic immigrants.

About 44 percent of adult Hispanic immigrants dropped out of school before getting their high-school diplomas, compared with about 15 percent of those born here. More than half of foreign-born Hispanic children who had dropped out of schools in their native lands never set foot in schools in the United States.

The Pew Hispanic Center has found that foreign-born Hispanic teenagers are more likely than other immigrants their age to have come to the United States to work rather than study. They earn a lot more money than black people and white people their age—a reflection of long hours rather than high pay—and they're a key source of low-skilled, low-wage labor for agriculture and other industries. Because the nation's immigration policies place a heavy emphasis on bringing in the family members of legal U.S. residents, the current influx of the poor and uneducated props open the door for immigration by people with similar backgrounds.

"America needs a highly educated work force, but we have an immigration policy that is importing huge numbers of undereducated immigrants," says David Ray, a spokesman for the Federation for American Immigration Reform, a nonprofit advocacy group in Washington. "You get a cheap, exploitable employee for the business owner, and an additional tax burden for the American worker."

When Hispanic families come here illegally, paying for college can be especially tough. Many states' public colleges require undocumented immigrants to pay the same comparatively high tuition as nonresidents, although a few states, including California, New York, and Texas, have agreed in recent years to let them pay in-state rates. They are ineligible for federal financial aid for college, and for many scholarships and grants awarded by colleges and private foundations.

"A lot of donors are uncomfortable about helping undocumented students," says Mr. Paredes of the Hispanic Scholarship Fund, which provided more than $26 million in aid to more than 7,500 Hispanic college students during the 2002–3 academic year.

The educational prospects improve substantially for the U.S.–born children of Hispanic immigrants, who account for about 28 percent of the total Hispanic population and attend college at the same rate as whites.

That is especially true of people whose families came here from the Dominican Republic. Ramona Hernandez, director of the Dominican Studies Institute at City College, in New York, says she believes, based on personal experience and anecdotes, that Dominican immigrants place an exceptionally high value on education.

"I used to show off my books on the train," says Ms. Hernandez. "I wanted people to see I was going to college. I wanted to share that information on the subway train as I was commuting from Lehman College to my home in the Bronx."

As with other immigrant groups, members of the so-called "second generation" of Hispanics—the U.S.–born children of the foreign-born—tend to have a fire in the belly that makes them achieve at levels that their own children, the "third generation," can't match. Among the U.S.–born children of U.S.–born Hispanics—the children of the "third generation" and beyond—just 36 percent of 18- to 24-year-old high-school graduates are in college. The second generation of Hispanics catches up with the white population in terms of college attendance, but its descendants lose some of that ground.

Moving into New States

About half of the nation's Hispanics live in just two states, California and Texas. Eight other states—Arizona, Colorado, Florida, Illinois, Nevada, New Jersey, New Mexico, and New York—account for more than a fourth.

But Hispanics also are rapidly moving into states where relatively few had lived just a few decades ago. During the 1990s, their numbers more than doubled in Kentucky, Minnesota, and Nebraska, more than tripled in Alabama, Tennessee, and South Carolina, and more than quadrupled in Arkansas, Georgia, and North Carolina.

Many colleges in these states are just beginning to find ways to serve Hispanic students.

FOR MANY HISPANICS, COLLEGE IS AN OBSTACLE COURSE

Hispanic high-school graduates are more likely to go on to college than their white peers, yet are less likely to earn bachelor's degrees. They are deterred by several obstacles tied to poverty and immigration, and others that they inadvertently create for themselves by focusing as hard on paying bills as they do on getting through college. Among the biggest obstacles:

- **Poor academic preparation.** On average, Hispanic students score 9 percent to 11 percent lower than white students on standardized college-admissions tests. More than one-fourth of Hispanics enter college needing remedial English courses, compared with one-tenth of white freshmen, and more than half need remedial mathematics, compared with less than one-third of their white peers. On average, Hispanic students' college grades are lower, and those who need to play catch-up generally end up taking longer to earn a degree.

- **Parents who never attended college.** More than two out of five Hispanic freshmen at four-year colleges are the first in their family to attend college, compared with about one out of five white freshmen. Those whose parents can't speak English are even less likely to get sound advice from their families about college.

- **Worries about tuition.** More than three-fourths of Hispanic freshmen at four-year colleges report having major concerns about paying for their education, compared with one-fifth of white freshmen. Hispanic students tend not to take advantage of all the financial aid that is available to them, particularly loans, which usually account for most of the available assistance.

- **Not transferring from two-year colleges.** About 40 percent of 18- to 24-year-old Hispanic college students are enrolled in two-year institutions, compared with 25 percent of black and 25 percent of white students. Of those who do not start at four-year institutions, 39 percent have no degree and have dropped out within four years. Of those who begin at four-year institutions, just 18 percent leave college without a degree within four years.

- **Enrolling in college part time.** About 25 percent of traditional-age Hispanic college students are enrolled part time, compared with 15 percent of white students. Part-time college students of any race or ethnicity are more likely than full-timers to drop out.

- **Enrolling later in life.** Among the traditional college-age population, 33 percent of Hispanic high-school graduates and 42 percent of white high-school graduates are enrolled in undergraduate programs. Traditional-age college students are more likely than older students to earn their baccalaureates and go on to earn advanced degrees. About 4 percent of Hispanic high-school graduates 25 and older are enrolled in undergraduate programs, making them twice as likely as their white counterparts to still be working toward undergraduate degrees at that age when they are more likely to have children and other responsibilities distracting them from their studies.

SOURCES: U.S. Census Bureau; U.S. Department of Education; Higher Education Research Institute at the University of California at Los Angeles; Inter-University Program for Latino Research; Pew Hispanic Center

Carl V. Patton, president of Georgia State University, says his institution established a Hispanic-student-services office last spring and is working to increase Hispanic enrollment, now at about 3 percent, to 8 percent to reflect the size of Georgia's Hispanic population.

"We have found that the way you get these students is from word of mouth," he says. "A stream of students starts to come from the good schools, and those students will tell other students."

In Minnesota, Minneapolis Community and Technical College has joined with U.S. Bancorps to set up a program that trains Hispanic bank employees, in response to a threefold increase in that city's Hispanic population during the 1990s. Phillip L. Davis, the two-year college's president, says the program is popular because it trains students for existing jobs and is not just based on "off-in-the-distance speculation about what the job market will look like." In some states, like California, Florida, Illinois, and Texas, public colleges are feeling top-down pressure to better serve Hispanic students as Hispanic legislators grow in number and flex more muscle.

For public colleges in those states, improving services for Hispanic students is becoming "a budget issue," says Gilbert Cárdenas, director of the Inter-University Program for Latino Research. "They realize that if they are going to get the support of the elected officials, they have to be more sensitive to the broader needs of the state."

The Bush administration has taken note of the educational problems of Hispanic Americans. Since 2001 it has increased federal spending on colleges classified as "Hispanic-serving" by about 36 percent, to $93 million. It has also overseen a $39 million, or roughly 64 percent, increase in spending on grants to colleges of education to prepare teachers to work with students who do not speak English at home.

In October 2001, President Bush signed an executive order establishing the President's Advisory Commission on Educational Excellence for Hispanic Americans. In a report issued last March, the panel warned: "Hispanics are not maximizing their income potential or developing financial security. This leads to lost tax revenues, lower rates of consumer spending, reduced per-capita savings, and increased social costs."

Among its recommendations, the commission urged the federal government to conduct much more research on the needs of Hispanic students; hold colleges accountable for improving Hispanic graduation rates; and undertake a nationwide public-awareness campaign aimed at helping Hispanic parents navigate the nation's education system.

Upon the release of the commission's report, Secretary of Education Roderick R. Paige said: "We're not letting any more Hispanic kids slip through the cracks. It's a disgrace. And it's going to stop."

Ronald Reagan, and every president since, worked with similar panels on Hispanic education, with mixed results. Mr. Yzaguirre, of the National Council of La Raza, resigned as the head of such a commission under President Bill Clinton because, he says, in six years not a single federal agency had complied with an executive order instructing them to provide the panel with an inventory of programs for Hispanic students. The report from the newest commission says that it, too, had trouble getting federal departments and agencies to provide basic information about their services to Hispanic students.

Such developments have made many Hispanic advocates cynical about the prospect of the federal government's bringing about real improvements any time soon.

"We don't need any more reports," says Lauro F. Cavazos, who worked with such panels as secretary of education under Presidents Reagan and George H. W. Bush.

"We know what the problem is," Mr. Cavazos says. "We know what the solutions are. There just has to be a will to do it, to bring about the change."

Bibliography

Books

Benson, Sonia G., ed. *The Hispanic American Almanac: A Reference Work on Hispanics in the United States.* Detroit, Mich.: Gale, 2003.

Burciaga, José Antonio. *Drink Cultura: Chicanismo.* Santa Barbara, Calif.: Capra Press, 1993.

Darder, Antonia, and Rodolfo D. Torres, eds. *The Latino Studies Reader: Culture, Economy, Society.* Malden, Mass.: Blackwell Publishers, 1998.

Darder, Antonia, et al., eds. *Latinos and Education: A Critical Reader.* New York: Routledge, 1997.

Dávila, Arlene M. *Latinos, Inc.: The Marketing and Making of a People.* Berkeley, Calif.: University of California Press, 2001.

Delgado, Richard, and Jean Stefancic. *The Latino/a Condition: A Critical Reader.* New York: New York University Press, 1998.

Fox, Geoffrey E. *Hispanic Nation: Culture, Politics, and the Constructing of Identity.* New York: Carol Pub., 1996.

González, Carolina, and Seth Kugel. *Nueva York: The Complete Guide to Latino Life in the Five Boroughs.* New York: St. Martin's Griffin, 2006.

González, Juan. *Harvest of Empire: A History of Latinos in America.* New York: Viking, 2000.

Gonzalez-Pando, Miguel. *The Cuban Americans.* Westport, Conn.: Greenwood Press, 1998.

Gracia, Jorge J. E., and Pablo De Greiff, eds. *Hispanics/Latinos in the United States: Ethnicity, Race, and Rights.* New York: Routledge, 2000.

Haslip-Viera, Gabriel, and Sherrie L. Baver, eds. *Latinos in New York: Communities in Transition.* Notre Dame, Ind.: University of Notre Dame Press, 1996.

Haslip-Viera, Gabriel, et al., eds. *Boricuas in Gotham: Puerto Ricans in the Making of New York City.* Princeton, N.J.: M. Wiener Publishers, 2004.

Heyck, Denis, ed. *Barrios and Borderlands: Cultures of Latinos and Latinas in the United States.* New York: Routledge, 1994.

Hunter, Miranda. *Latino Americans and Immigration Laws: Crossing the Border.* Philadelphia, Pa.: Mason Crest Publishers, 2006.

———. *The Story of Latino Civil Rights: Fighting for Justice.* Philadelphia, Pa.: Mason Crests Publishers, 2006.

Judis, John B., and Ruy Teixeira. *The Emerging Democratic Majority.* New York: Scribner, 2002.

Milkman, Ruth. *L.A. Story: Immigrant Workers and the Future of the U.S. Labor Movement.* New York: R. Sage Foundation, 2006.

Morales, Ed. *Living in Spanglish: The Search for Latino Identity in America.* New York: St. Martin's Press, 2002.

Portes, Alejandro, and Alex Stepick. *City on the Edge: The Transformation of Miami.* Berkeley, Calif.: University of California Press, 1993.

Ramos, Jorge. *The Latino Wave: How Hispanics Will Elect the Next American President.* New York: Rayo, 2004.

———. *The Other Face of America: Chronicles of the Immigrants Shaping Our Future.* New York: Rayo, 2002.

Rodriguez, Richard. *Brown: The Last Discovery of America.* New York: Viking, 2002.

Sánchez, José Ramón. *Boricua Power: A Political History of Puerto Ricans in the United States.* New York: New York University Press, 2007.

Soto, Teresa J. *Marketing to Hispanics: A Strategic Approach to Assessing and Planning Your Initiative.* Chicago: Dearborn Trade Pub., 2006.

Suro, Roberto. *Remembering the American Dream: Hispanic Immigration and National Policy.* New York: Twentieth Century Fund Press, 1994.

———. *Strangers Among Us: How Latino Immigration Is Transforming America.* New York: Alfred A. Knopf, 1998.

Stavans, Ilan. *The Hispanic Condition: Reflections on Culture and Identity in America.* New York: HarperCollins, 1995.

Stavans, Ilan, and Harold Augenbraum, eds. *Encyclopedia Latina: History, Culture, and Society in the United States.* Danbury, Conn.: Grolier Academic Reference, 2005.

Suárez-Orozco, Marcelo M., and Mariela M. Páez, eds. *Latinos: Remaking America.* Berkeley, Calif.: University of California Press, 2002.

Tatum, Charles M. *Chicano Popular Culture: Que Hable el Peublo.* Tucson, Ariz.: University of Arizona Press, 2001.

Torres-Saillant, Silvio, and Ramona Hernández. *The Dominican Americans.* Westport, Conn.: Greenwood Press, 1998.

Vigil, James Diego. *From Indians to Chicanos: The Dynamics of Mexican-American Culture.* Prospect Heights, Ill.: Waveland Press, 1998.

Web Sites

Readers seeking additional information about Hispanic Americans may wish to refer to the following Web sites, all of which were operational as of this writing.

Center for Puerto Rican Studies

centropr.org

Part of Hunter College, a division of the City University of New York (CUNY), the Center for Puerto Rican Studies seeks to acquire, preserve, and disseminate materials relating to Puerto Rican culture and history.

Cuban American National Council, Inc.

www.cnc.org

The CNC studies the Cuban-American population and provides educational, housing, and employment services to those in need, regardless of ethnicity.

The Domincan American National Roundtable (DANR)

www.danr.org

Devoted to improving the quality of life of all Dominican Americans, DANR conducts research and policy analysis.

El Boricua

www.elboricua.com

Founded in 1995, *El Boricua* is a monthly online magazine that seeks to preserve and promote Puerto Rican culture and history.

Hispanic Online

www.hispaniconline.com

Owned and operated by Hispanic Publishing Associates, which produces *Hispanic* magazine and *Hispanic Trends* magazine, Hispanic Online provides a wealth of online news, entertainment, and other information for Latinos.

League of United Latin American Citizens (LULAC)

www.lulac.org

According to its Web site, LULAC is the oldest and largest Latino association in the United States. With over 700 councils throughout the country, the organization focuses on bettering the educational and economic prospects of Hispanics while safeguarding their civil rights.

Mexican American Legal Defense Fund (MALDEF)

www.maldef.org

The leading Latino civil rights organization, MALDEF was founded in 1968 in San Antonio, Texas. Currently based in Los Angeles, California, MALDEF works to integrate Hispanic Americans into U.S. society through advocacy, education, and litigation.

National Council of La Raza (NCLR)

www.nclr.org

Founded in 1968, the NCLR is the largest Latino civil rights organization in the country. Combining research with advocacy and policy analysis, the NCLR and its affiliates seek to improve opportunities for Hispanic Americans.

National Puerto Rican Coalition, Inc. (NPRC)

www.bateylink.org

Founded in 1977, the NPRC seeks to improve the social, economic, and political health of the Puerto Rican community in the United States and in Puerto Rico itself.

Additional Periodical Articles with Abstracts

More information about Hispanic Americans and related subjects can be found in the following articles. Readers who require a more comprehensive selection are advised to consult the *Readers' Guide Abstracts* and other H.W. Wilson Publications.

Dismantling the Language Barrier. Tim Porter. *American Journalism Review* v. 25 pp48–54 October/November 2003.

In an attempt to break into the Hispanic market, major newspaper corporations are spending money on new and expanded Spanish-language editions, Porter reports. The Hispanic community is America's biggest ethnic group and the fastest-growing sector of the nation's economy, but many of its members are unable to read, or choose not to read, mainstream newspapers in English. Disappointed by their inability to increase circulation through traditional methods and inspired by the successes of *El Nuevo Herald* and *Hoy*, mainstream publishers are launching Spanish-language titles. This year, Tribune Co., Belo Corp., and Knight Ridder have established daily Spanish-language papers, committing millions of dollars and dozens of employees to them.

Mongrel America. Gregory Rodriguez. *Atlantic Monthly* (1993) v. 291 pp95–7 January/February 2003.

The most important long-term social fact in the United States may be the increasing rates of intermarriage among members of different ethnic and racial groups, the author writes. Research by the Population Research Center, in Portland, Oregon, predicts that the black intermarriage rate will rise dramatically during this century; by 2100, 37 percent of African Americans will claim mixed ancestry. By century's end the number of Latinos claiming mixed ancestry will be more than twice the number claiming a single background. The immigrants of recent decades are helping to create a new American identity, and this identity is emerging not due to politics or any specific public policies but because of powerful underlying cultural forces.

Inventing Hispanics: A Diverse Minority Resists Being Labeled. Amitai Etzioni. *Brookings Review* v. 20 pp10–13 Winter 2002.

Some observers fear that efforts to group Hispanics into a single ethnic category are dividing American society along racial lines, Etzioni contends. However, these efforts are having little impact, as Hispanics see themselves as Americans rather than a distinct minority. Based on the recent past, Hispanics will continue to create and re-create American society as a community of communities, not of racially divided subgroups.

Did Hispanics Really Surge to Bush? Richard S. Dunham. *Business Week* p51 November 29, 2004.

Though many believe President George W. Bush received an impressive 44 percent of the Hispanic vote in the recent election, up significantly from the 35 percent he garnered in 2000, a *Business Week* study suggests his gains were more modest, Dunham observes. The survey looked at real election returns from 62 jurisdictions in 13 states, predominantly places where Hispanics accounted for 75 to 95 percent of the population, and found that the president improved on his 2000 performance in 85 percent of these heavily Hispanic areas, undercutting Democrats' claims that his share of the vote had not improved. Nonetheless, Bush's gains averaged a mere 3 percentage points, considerably less than the 9-point jump Republicans have been celebrating.

Jump Starting Latino Achievement. Ronald Roach. *Diverse: Issues in Higher Education* v. 23 pp26–9 September 21, 2006.

The writer reports on some dedicated scholars and programs that are working to close the achievement gap between Latino students and other students.

The Americano Dream. *The Economist* v. 376 pp8–9 July 16, 2005.

According to the author, many are concerned that Hispanic immigrants entering the U.S. will divide the nation into two groups, an English-speaking majority and a Spanish-speaking subgroup. The reality is that legal immigrants are actually helping to counteract such divisive forces. They have done this in part by settling in the cities that domestic migrants are leaving and then dispersing to other areas, thus allaying fears that Hispanics will congregate in giant ghettos. Furthermore, Hispanic second and third-generation Hispanics are either bilingual or mainly English-speaking and are moving into the political mainstream. In addition, many are marrying outside their ethnic background.

Fighting the Latino Dropout Rate. Michelle Adam. *The Education Digest* v. 68 pp23–7 February 2003.

In an article condensed from the December 16, 2002, issue of *The Hispanic Outlook in Higher Education*, Adam discusses the struggle to reduce the large number of Latinos dropping out of high school. The Latino dropout rate is greater than that of African Americans and whites. Rogelio Saenz, a professor of sociology at Texas A&M University, claims that this is due to such factors as academic expectations and performance, accelerated role-taking, generational status and acculturation, and adversarial structures. The Carlos Cantu Hispanic Education and Opportunity Endowment hopes to address the issue of Latino dropout rates, which has become a leading priority for the Texas Educational Excellence Project (TEEP). TEEP president Ken Meier wishes to use the endowment to study the issue throughout the United States, ultimately connecting with other researchers and schools and cross-pollinating research and policies by means of the TEEP's Web site.

Hispanic Growth. Anne C. Lewis. *The Education Digest* v. 71 pp71–2 March 2006.

Research by the Pew Hispanic Center and other studies have established that the Hispanic population in the United States is soaring, and the population's young age profile presents interesting challenges for public schools nationwide, Lewis reports. The Pew study of six Southern states revealed that the number of Hispanics increased by more than 300 percent on average in the last decade. It also found that the early immigrant population is composed mostly of young men, who eventually start or bring in families, meaning that the full effect of Hispanic immigration is only starting to be felt in public school enrollments.

Soccer, Salsa, and Stereotypes. Mirela Roncevic. *Library Journal* v. 130 p122 July 2005.

An interview with Ilan Stavans, main editor of the four-volume *Encyclopedia Latina: History, Culture, and Society in the United States*, is provided. Stavans discusses Che Guevara, Latino food, the growth of the Hispanic population in the U.S., what books best portray the reality of Latino life in the U.S., soccer and baseball among Latinos, the areas of American life where Latinos are underrepresented, and how unflattering Latino stereotypes can be overcome.

Fear of a Brown Planet. Roberto Lovato. *The Nation* v. 278 pp17–18+ June 28, 2004.

According to Lovato, a new wave of white minority Republican politics is beginning to have an effect in California. Proponents of this new politics of fear, which is predominantly a California phenomenon but is cropping up across the United States, are redefining who is a racial victim and who a racial oppressor, neatly inverting—and co-opting—the arguments and terms of the civil rights movement. Driven by fears of a Latino takeover, these Republicans are fighting against the Movimiento Estudiantil Chicano de Aztlan, known as MEChA, a national Chicano student group founded during the identity and power movements of the early 1970s.

Hard Times in the Big Easy. Gary Younge. *The Nation* v. 282 p10 March 13, 2006.

Americans apparently love immigration but detest immigrants, which is precisely the contradiction now unfolding in the rebuilding of New Orleans, Younge observes. Since Hurricane Katrina, the city's Hispanic population has soared from 3 percent to an estimated 30 percent, and every morning at Lee Circle hundreds of day laborers come together to wait for work. Meanwhile, in a speech to business owners and contractors, New Orleans mayor Ray Nagin stated that he knew they were concerned that the city would be overrun by Mexican laborers. Nagin's words were crude, but his behavior has been consistent with a mind-set in which Hispanic migrant workers are both vital and criminalized, encouraged and exploited, accepted and abused.

Latinos Rise Nationwide. A. R. Williams. *National Geographic* v. 204 pp24–26 November 2003.

Latinos have overtaken African-Americans as the largest minority in America, Williams observes. Numbering 38.8 million, Latinos now represent 13 percent of America's demographic total. With high birth rates and legal and illegal immigration increasing their numbers, Latinos have more than doubled their presence in the United States in the last 20 years and added 3.5 million to their count since the 2000 census. In regions where they are most populous—the West and Southwest and the cities of New York, Miami, and Chicago—Latinos have already had an effect on local culture. Now, as they follow jobs and lifestyles into the American heartland, they are transforming the fabric of the entire nation. Graphs and maps present Latino population statistics.

The Hispanic Republic of Texas. John J. Miller. *National Review* v. 54 pp32+ October 14, 2002.

The most important political trend of the next decade or so in the state of Texas will be the ascendancy of the Democrats due to the growth of the Hispanic population, Miller believes. Texas is home to some of the oldest and most established Mexican-American communities in the nation, as well as plenty of newcomers; indeed, the state's Hispanic population numbers 6.7 million. Although Texas Hispanics are more conservative than most other Hispanics, two-thirds regard themselves as Democrats and in this respect are not much different from the national Hispanic profile. According to Miller, more Hispanic voters will in the future translate into fewer Republican wins.

The Return of the Native: The Past Meets the Future in Mestizo America. Richard Rodriguez. *New Perspectives Quarterly* v. 23 pp21–2 Summer 2006.

According to Rodriguez, contemporary America confronts the return of the Native. The Indian had seemingly vanished from U.S. history, but abruptly, people who were meant to no longer exist are spilling out from over the southern horizon. Americans have decided to dub these immigrants Hispanics in reference to the Spanish king who once ruled Mexico and the American Southwest, but the majority of them are people of mixed blood, or mestizos. Ultimately, Rodriguez writes, these mestizos bring to America a sense of impurity because their gift is that they are a people who violate borders.

The Latino Giant Awakes. Andrew Stephen. *New Statesman* v. 135 pp30–1 May 1, 2006.

The growing political and economic power of Hispanic immigrants in the U.S. has created an ugly mood of racism, with undocumented "illegals" accused of taking American jobs, housing, and health care, Stephen reports. The situation presents a dilemma for the country's political leaders, who need to balance white Republican voters' desire for legislated surveillance and tighter border controls with the demands of capitalism for illegal cheap labor as well as legal technology experts from India. A second immigration issue is purely political: Although a significant proportion of newcomers to the country cannot vote because they are illegal, the registered Hispanic vote is of vital importance to Republicans and Democrats alike. The ironies of the racism directed at America's Latino population are discussed.

L.I. Clash on Immigrants Is Gaining Political Force. Patrick Healy. *The New York Times* ppA1+ November 29, 2004.

A new wave of Hispanic immigrants has swept over Long Island's historically white suburban hamlets, Healy observes. As complaints increase, politicians are responding with crackdowns and new laws. Residents are furious about overcrowded homes and lines of day laborers in their towns. A proposal is being floated to deputize some police officers, giving them the power to detain people found to be in the country illegally.

For Younger Latinos, a Shift to Smaller Families. Mireya Navarro. *The New York Times* pp1+ December 5, 2004.

According to Navarro, Hispanic-American women are choosing to have smaller families, in some cases resisting the social pressures that shaped the Hispanic tradition of big families. Latinos became the country's largest minority party because they had the highest fertility rate among the major ethnic groups. But that fertility rate is on the decline as more women work at a younger age, achieve higher levels of education, and postpone marriage, all of which affect when and how often they give birth, say sociologists who study Hispanic trends.

For Latinos in the Midwest, a Time to Be Heard. Randal C. Archibold. *The New York Times* ppA1+ April 25, 2006.

A rally in Liberal, Kansas, by pro-immigration forces produced a turnout of over 800 people, mostly Hispanic Americans, Archibold reports. This demonstration provides evidence of the political activism that the immigration issue is generating, even in the rural areas of the Midwest. The Midwest became a destination for Hispanic Americans in the 1980s when they came to work in the region's meatpacking industries. There is still a lot of resentment towards illegal aliens in this part of the country but attitudes are slowly changing.

Bridging a Racial Rift That Isn't Black and White. Rachel L. Swarns. *The New York Times* pA1+ October 3, 2006.

For centuries, the South has been defined by the color line and the struggle for accommodation between blacks and whites, Swarns maintains. But the arrival of thousands of Hispanic immigrants over the past decade is quietly changing the dynamics of race relations in many Southern towns. The article profiles Willacoochee, Georgia, an immigrant boomtown in Atkinson County, about 45 miles north of the Florida border. Blacks, who had settled into a familiar, if sometimes uneasy, relationship with whites, are outnumbered by Hispanics. The two groups live and work side by side and compete fiercely for working-class jobs and government resources. By several estimates, blacks are already losing ground. The jobless rate for black men in Georgia is triple that of Hispanic men, and more blacks than Hispanics fail to meet minimum standards in Atkinson County public schools. Many blacks express anguish at being supplanted by immigrants who know little of their history and sometimes treat them with disdain as they fill factory jobs, buy property, open small businesses, and scale the economic ladder.

The Battle for Latino Souls. Arian Campo-Flores. *Newsweek* v. 145 pp50–1 March 21, 2005.

According to Campo-Flores, Pentecostal churches in the United States are using savvy marketing to lure Hispanics. Although Hispanics are predominantly Catholic, research shows that the longer they are in the United States, the more open they are to other faiths. This has prompted all religions to court Hispanics with marketing strategies more often associated with corporate America. The competition is particularly fierce among Pentecostals, whose cathartic, music-filled worship style and aggressive proselytizing have proved particularly attractive to Hispanic communities. The writer discusses how Pentecostal churches in Chicago are battling for Hispanic members.

That Latino Show. Juleyka Lantigua. *The Progressive* v. 67 pp32–3 February 2003.

The writer discusses the growth in the Latino television audience and the types of roles given to Latino actors on television.

Viva la Diferencia. Jan Jarboe Russell. *Texas Monthly* v. 32 pp68+ June 2004.

The future of a predominantly Hispanic Texas is less likely to reflect the fears of Harvard professor Samuel Huntington and more likely to resemble San Antonio, Russell contends. In "The Hispanic Challenge," an article that appeared in the March-April issue of *Foreign Policy*, Huntington argues that Hispanic, and particularly Mexican, immigrants are not assimilating into U.S. culture. This, he believes, will create the most serious racial division in the United States since the battle between blacks and whites. San Antonio, which is already 58 percent Mexican American, enjoys a culture that is both more hopeful and more complicated than the one Huntington describes, however. According to Russell, Huntington ignores the fact that a shared border creates common interests as well as conflicts.

Grand Opportunity Party: Hispanic Americans and the Republican Party. Jan Jarboe Russell. *Texas Monthly* v. 33 pp80+ March 2005.

With the help of Lionel Sosa, the head of a San Antonio advertising agency that specializes in marketing to Hispanics, George W. Bush has won a record share of the Hispanic vote in Texas, Russell reports. Democrats have been counting on the ever-growing Hispanic population to make them competitive in Texas and throughout the United States, but Republicans believe that Sosa's culturally conservative, American-dream-oriented message can help them capture a significant fraction of the Hispanic vote and solidify their majority status. Sometime around 2030, when the Democratic dream of a majority Hispanic Texas becomes a reality, the Democrats may find themselves unable to change the direction of Texas politics if they fail to change their stand-by-your-party message.

Se Habla Espanol. Oscar Cesares. *Texas Monthly* v. 33 pp94+ June 2005.

The writer reflects on the fact that, as a third-generation Mexican American raised in Texas, it is natural that he speaks better English than Spanish, but many Latinos expect him to speak Spanish perfectly, and Anglos expect his English to be just as good.

Why Juan Can't Read: Bilingual Education Programs. Patricia Kilday Hart. *Texas Monthly* v. 34 pp104+ October 2006.

Bilingual education programs across the state of Texas are failing to teach English to Hispanic children, Hart reports. Two years ago, more than eight out of ten seventh and eighth-graders with limited English skills failed the Texas Assessment of Knowledge and Skills test, despite extensive bilingual and English-as-a-second-language programs. The Mexican American Legal Defense and Educational Fund argues that since 2003, the Texas Education Agency has not properly audited those programs. Critics also contend that overreliance on Spanish in bilingual programs actually slows the learning of English by Spanish-speaking students. A major obstacle is a shortage of qualified elementary school bilingual education and English-as-a-second-language teachers. This lack of teachers forces districts to prematurely push students out of bilingual programs and into English-only classes to make space for newcomers. The writer discusses a promising "dual language" approach at Del Valle High School, in El Paso, that delivers far better results.

Under the Sun: Effects of the New Wave of Hispanic Immigrants. Liz Halloran. *U.S. News & World Report* v. 138 pp20–25 June 20, 2005.

An influx of Mexican immigrants is transforming communities throughout the United States, Halloran observes. Waves of undocumented immigrants, mainly from Mexico, are pouring into states that have little experience with large-scale immigration. Bitter disputes—fueled by talk radio, new interest groups, and a yearning for a more simple past—have hounded the new immigrants in states such as Georgia, Utah, Tennessee, and Arizona. No state is struggling with immigration as much as North Carolina, however, where the Latino population, which is largely made up of undocumented immigrants, has soared by 400 percent over 15 years. A harsh war of words has broken out over the increase, which has been driven by the lure of agriculture, poultry processing, and unskilled-labor jobs, as well as by a surplus of work created by a building boom.

Land of Opportunity. Mortimer B. Zuckerman. *U.S. News & World Report,* v. 138 p64 June 20, 2005.

The high numbers of Hispanic immigrants who are entering the United States should be regarded as an opportunity rather than a problem, Zuckerman claims. Some Americans—perhaps driven by nativist, anti-immigrant sentiment or fears about the cost of illegal immigrants—condemn the massive waves of legal and illegal Hispanic immigration into the U.S. over the last 50 years. These immigrants are largely from Mexico, and the fear is that Hispanics will retain their language and culture, staying separate from the rest of the country. Nonetheless, Hispanics are learning English as quickly as any immigrant group, and are intermarrying at the similar rates. Every new wave of immigrants has enriched America's culture, and the evidence strongly suggests that the country can absorb Hispanics, just as it did earlier generations from Europe, and weave them into a dynamic American society.

The New Border Wars: Views of Samuel P. Huntington. *The Wilson Quarterly* v. 28 p97 Summer 2004.

This article is adapted from "The Hispanic Challenge," by Samuel P. Huntington, which appeared in the March-April 2004 *Foreign Policy*, along with criticisms of his views, which appeared in the May-June 2004 issue.

Index

DATE DUE

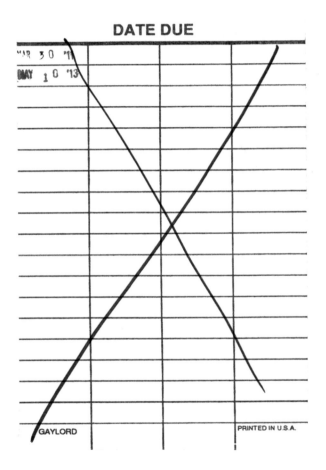